The Finger of God

A Practical Manual for Deliverance Ministry

By Torace D. Solomon

DEDICATION

This book is dedicated to the memory of my grandfather, Pastor Horace Solomon Sr. Thank you for being a great dad! Your legacy lives on through me! I will always be real with God because of you!

Foreword

I want to personally recommend The Finger of God by Torace Solomon. This brand new book will give you fresh insight and revelation concerning the ministry of deliverance. Deliverance is oftentimes overlooked, mistreated or rejected. Torace unravels misconceptions about this ministry and its functions. Helping believers all around the world to walk free from cycles of dysfunction, generational curses, and soul ties.

As a believer you will receive impartation, and revelation on how to engage the enemy in times of uncertainty. The devil wants to destroy your hope, future and ability to contend against his army. Torace places an emphasis on how to break legal ground, break word curses, and pray against the attacks of the enemy. Giving practical tools to overcome the snares from the enemy.

I have been involved in deliverance ministry for over 35 years and I am certain that as you read this book you will receive understanding, visitations and be equipped for the work of the ministry.

It is my prayer that every believers walks in liberty and is not held back by the enemy. I want to encourage believers from around the world to get this book in the hands of other believers, churches and organizations as a tool to equip and establish a strong foundation on the ministry of deliverance.

Torace Solomon is not just a strong prophet. He is an amazing person and gift to those who meet him. Torace's love for the supernatural and righteousness makes him incredibly valuable for this generation. It is my prayer that this book would get on the hands of believers around the world.

Apostle John Eckhardt

Endorsements

The Finger of God: A Practical Manual for Deliverance Ministry is an essential tool for Believers that intercede, heal the sick and desire a strong ministry in deliverance. Every Believer has been called to Set the Captive Free. In this book, Torace Solomon strongly communicates the necessity for deliverance and the practical steps to obtaining it and bringing freedom to others. In my opinion. I believe that this book carries the answers to what we, the Church, will face in the days ahead. Let's rise in authority and power!

Yolanda Stith, God's Friend
Lead Pastor at ANWA Baltimore
Host, Junia's Table Live with Yolanda Stith
Author of Invisible Battlegrounds and Jael's Tent

Endorsements

In this deliverance manual Prophet Torace Soloman demystifies the crucial ministry of deliverance and provides in depth insight on the subject. You will be both equipped and enlightened as you read this profound teaching. Churches and ministry centers everywhere will benefit from this vital tool. Hungry believers will find new levels of freedom and receive deliverance ministry training through this work.

Ryan LeStrange,
Author of Breaking Curses

Table of Contents

Introduction

The ministry of deliverance is one of the most misrepresented ministries in the modern church. Most churches today view this ministry as dramatic and unnecessary. They try to numb the symptoms of demonic oppression with exciting sermons and declarations of financial turnaround. They have replaced the need for radical spiritual encounters with never-ending praise breaks. While praise is a powerful tool for breakthrough, it should never be confused with or replace the ministry of deliverance. On the other hand, we have churches that operate in deliverance to some extent, but they are so judgmental and religious that it makes people ashamed to need freedom.

Joel 2:32 (KJV)
32 And it shall come to pass, that whosoever shall call on the name of the Lord shall be delivered: for in mount Zion and in Jerusalem shall be deliverance, as the Lord hath said, and in the remnant whom the Lord shall call.

Deliverance is for EVERYONE who chooses to call upon the name of the Lord! The church is the only entity in the world that has been given authority over the kingdom of darkness, and that authority came directly from the Head of the church— our Lord and Savior Jesus Christ. He exercised deliverance regularly, and people marveled at His authority over unclean spirits. This is what set Him apart from the other teachers of His time! In the Bible, we never see the authority to command demons prior to Jesus' ministry. His ability to demand peace in the lives of the oppressed gave Him the influence He needed to expand the kingdom of God. He is the blueprint for every deliverance minister. Jesus was sent from heaven to deliver people from the influence of darkness. He was anointed to proclaim deliverance to the captives.

Luke 4:18 (KJV)

18 The Spirit of the Lord is upon Me, because He hath anointed Me to preach the gospel to the poor; He hath sent me to heal the brokenhearted, to preach deliverance to the captives, and recovering of sight to the blind, to set at liberty them that are bruised,

The reason that deliverance ministry hasn't been embraced by many churches is because people have stopped following Jesus' practices. They have stopped using the authority that Jesus gave and try to cast out demons by their own intelligence. Deliverance is a ministry of GRACE, meaning that it can only happen through divine intervention. Human intellect is not enough to get people to breakthrough. We must cast out demons with the authority of heaven.

Luke 11:20 (AMP)

20 But if I drive out the demons by the finger of God, then the kingdom of God has already come upon you.

In this passage, Jesus was in a debate against the Pharisees about the source of His authority to cast out demons, and I believe His response to these accusations gives us the overall mission for every deliverance minister. To cast out demons by the finger of God means to command them to leave by His power. When deliverance is done correctly, the kingdom of God is expanded. That raises a question: what is the kingdom of God? Paul answered this question in the book of Romans.

Romans 14:17 (AMP)

17 for the kingdom of God is not a matter of eating and drinking [what one likes], but of righteousness and peace and joy in the Holy Spirit.

Deliverance brings people into righteousness, peace, and joy. Demonic influences come to keep people from righteousness because they want us to live shameful and unclean lives. They don't want us to have peace, so they do everything possible to keep us in a place of fear and torment. Finally, the ministry of deliverance brings joy! The kingdom of darkness wants us to be miserable and depressed because demons know that supernatural joy is our strength. True deliverance brings us into our kingdom identity.

People are skeptical of deliverance ministry because so many ministers become extremists and flock to the altars to validate the areas in their soul that have voids. One regrettable side effect of unscriptural practices in deliverance is that scriptural teachings are sometimes thrown out as well because of the terror ensued by dramatic antics. Fear has stopped us from hitting demonic oppression head-on. The practice of casting out demons is not a luxury. It is a necessity for sanctification and kingdom advancement, for it's the responsibility of every believer. A well-known deliverance minister and theologian in the 1970-1990s was Derrick Prince. He taught that you are not effectively advancing the kingdom if you fear casting out devils. He gave me much of my foundational understanding of deliverance.

Fear gripped the early American church by the allegations of witchcraft in 16th and 17th century England and 17th century America. In England, it was reported that children vomited articles which allegedly proved demonic possession. Then, in 1692, Cotton Mather, an extremist Boston preacher who graduated from Harvard with honors, roused the people of Salem, Massachusetts against witches. Due to the testimony of several children, 19 people were hanged, and 150 were imprisoned after being accused of demon possession. In the presence of the accused, these children would throw "fits" and would go into what seemed to be a trance. They would name people whom they said were responsible for their torment. Though many of the accused showed a spirit and faith worthy of martyrs, judges who were men of integrity pronounced them guilty. As a result of the publicity surrounding these trials, Americans of that day turned away from the supernatural and branded all that the Bible teaches about Satan and demons as superstition. This brand of the supernatural has continued into the modern church all because one knowledgeable teacher became an extremist, which led to the death and destruction of families. We must be careful not to allow a passion for deliverance to turn into a dangerous obsession.

Many deliverance ministers have fallen into the extremist category and make it scary for deliverance to flow freely in churches. They conduct screaming contests with demons around the altar, and they allow demons to manifest and hurt people. They teach unscriptural practices that lead to chaos and end up wondering why their ministries won't grow. Deliverance done properly has the potential to grow any church. However, it has become a ministry that people won't participate in because it can get "messy." It disturbs me to see people try to use deliverance to show off their "strength." That's not what deliverance ministry is about; deliverance ministry is a ministry of love! Jesus, operating in His role as a deliverance minister, used the authority from His Father to bring order to chaotic moments, not to prove His strength.

These self-sufficient types of practices have led people into deceptions about who can cast out demons. Holy Ghost-filled believers have been deceived into believing that only super anointed, perfect people can operate in deliverance. We have restricted deliverance to the Apostles and Pastors, and this is exactly what the enemy wants. He wants his kingdom to remain as hidden as possible. His goal is to influence God's people from the shadows. He doesn't want you to know that you have the finger of God to drive him from your life and the lives of anyone who accepts the abundant life that Christ offers.

In Mark, Jesus declared that the first hallmark of His followers would be the ability to cast out devils.

Mark 16:17 (AMP)

17And these signs shall follow them that believe; In My name shall they cast out devils; they shall speak with new tongues;

This short passage should debunk every myth that any self-centered, power-hungry, fear-spreading leader tries to indoctrinate you with. If you believe in Jesus Christ enough to submit to His teachings, then you have authority over the powers of hell!

We see time and time throughout scripture that you share your authority with whatever you come in agreement with. So, when Christ came and offered the gift of salvation, your decision to agree with that also enabled you to share in His authority as a child of God.

Romans 8:17 (AMP)

17 And if [we are His] children, [then we are His] heirs also: heirs of God and fellow heirs with Christ [sharing His spiritual blessing and inheritance], if indeed we share in His suffering so that we may also share in His glory.

The enemy knows this principle, so he works very hard to get you to agree with his lies. He wants the authority that God has reserved for you! He wants to keep as many people as possible ignorant to the power they have over his kingdom, so he bombards us with lies and deceit from the day we are born. He starts early and won't stop until you stop him.

This book is designed to guide and equip you to become an effective and strategic deliverance minister. You should be warned that deliverance ministry is an offensive weapon in the war against the kingdom of darkness. Once you step up to the plate, you will be attacked by hell on another level, but remember you have the authority to overcome it!

My Experience

I have been operating in deliverance ministry for well over 15 years. I haven't always known the terminologies, but I was born with a strong sensitivity to things of the spirit. As a child, I was tormented by demons, so I was terrified of them for a long time. They gave me nightmares and tried to train me to live a life of fear. Demons would come into my room as a child, and I would see them crawl on the walls. They would chase me in my dreams and speak to me during the night. Once I was freed from their torment, I became aggressive about making them leave God's people alone!

A major part of the reason that demons had so much access to my life was because of the generational sin of witchcraft and clairvoyance that ran deep in my family line. Satan's plan for my life was for me to become a warlock like so many other men in my bloodline. Throughout my life, witches have tried to convince me to embrace the "gift" that was on my life. I'm not talking about imaginary Miss Cleo clairvoyance. It is real! For generations, my ancestors were documented in newspapers, police reports, and other public records as faith healers, tarot card readers, and seers that produced results and made a fortune from their ability to see into the spiritual realm.

My ancestors didn't have normal jobs. They weren't cleaning other people's houses, raising other people's children, or working other people's farms like most African-American people during that time. In the early 1900s, my ancestors were buying houses and land with the money that came from capitalizing off the spirit of divination. They were widely known, and they used the "gift" to obtain affluence and influence.

The enemy wanted me to continue on that path, and I was intrigued quite honestly. I grew up in a spiritually charged atmosphere. As a child, I gravitated to books about invoking spirits, incense, and spiritual visitations. I was always too afraid to try anything, but if I hadn't been raised by sanctified parents and grandparents, I would probably be a very rich warlock today. Satan thought that through torment and promises of wealth that he could prevent me from becoming the passionate deliverance minister I am today.

Soon after salvation, I learned about my authority over the enemy and the torment stopped. One of my most vibrant memories about deliverance began during my freshman year of college. I joined a campus ministry and somehow ended up as the Director of Prayer and Intercession. One night as I was leading prayer, one of our students fell to the floor and began to squirm like a snake and hiss. I froze because I knew exactly what was going on, and my mind automatically went to a place of fear. I was scared to touch him. I didn't want to live through that torment again. Everyone in the room panicked and looked at me. The Holy Spirit came upon me in a way that I had not felt before and have not felt since. I laid my hands on his stomach, and he immediately began to cough up a greenish fluid. At that point, I had not read any books on deliverance. I didn't know anything about demon groupings or legal rights, but I did know the voice of God and how to pray. That night, he gave his life to the Lord and was filled with the Holy Spirit and prayed in tongues. That experience was the first of the many scuffles I've had with the kingdom of darkness!

My beliefs about deliverance are very simple. Deliverance is not rocket science! There are so many erroneous and extreme teachings about deliverance floating around. In my opinion, they give way too much information and too much credit to the kingdom of darkness.

If you aren't careful, deliverance ministry can easily give room for legalism. Deliverance is something that happens by the love and grace of God. It doesn't follow one script or one formula. The enemy is a legalist; God isn't. I believe that it is dangerous to spend more time studying and learning the enemy's legalistic tactics than learning how to express the grace and love of God to help people become free. Strong deliverance ministers don't study demons; they study people.

I have seen so many deliverance ministers go to the extreme, trying to make everything a demonic manifestation. They become so learned and studied in paganism and occult lore that they forget the importance of time in God's presence. Deliverance is a ministry that should be Holy Spirit led, which means that the deliverance minister should spend as much time learning the habits of the Holy Spirit as possible. Knowing how the enemy operates is vital, but your knowledge should never trump the leading of the Spirit! He is so much smarter than we are.

The objective of this book is to teach you how to drive out every negative force influencing your life by the finger of God so that His kingdom can come upon your life in a greater measure! This book will give you guidelines and information to help you learn as much from the Holy Spirit as possible. This won't happen overnight. You can't read your way into it. Your effectiveness will grow as you submit to God.

Deliverance ministry is not for the faint of heart. The kingdom of hell is highly organized and strategic in its attacks. You must prepare for battle. In the chapters to come, I will teach you how to protect yourself from these attacks. Don't be afraid; Jesus wants you to know how to evict the devil. He wants to crush the kingdom of darkness under the feet of those who choose to worship Him. You can do it! Going forward, you will have to become self-objective and honest about any area in your life that is not submitted to God. The first step in becoming a deliverance minister is sweeping around your own front door. Prepare to be challenged to unearth hidden things and deal with unhealed hurts, unmet needs, and unresolved issues. It's time to bring your healing full circle, so you can extend the finger of God to those in need of breakthrough around you.

Chapter One
Your Authority

If you want to be an effective deliverance minister, you must have an unshakable understanding of your authority and where it comes from. It is impossible to cast out demons by the finger of God if you do not believe and submit to the authority of God. The only way that we can legally break the contracts of hell is through the authority of heaven. In the beginning, when God made us in His image and His likeness, He gave us authority. When God placed Adam in the garden of Eden, Satan and his followers had already been cast down to the earth from heaven. I'm sure Satan thought that he would rule earth since he couldn't be like God and rule the heavens. Genesis tells us that the world was chaotic and without form or order; in the beginning, then God decided to expand the glory of His kingdom even further. He created man with His hands and breathed His breath into him. He gave man dominion over the earth itself and everything on it.

Genesis 1:26 (AMP)

*26 Then God said, "Let Us (Father, Son, Holy Spirit) make man in Our image, according to Our likeness [not physical, but a spiritual personality and moral likeness]; and let them have complete authority over the fish of the sea, the birds of the air, the cattle, and over the entire earth, and over **everything** that creeps and crawls on the earth."*

From the beginning, we see when a man is submitted to God, he has dominion over the enemy! Somehow, Satan fell into the "everything that creeps and crawls" category. The bible tells us that the serpent was a beast of the field. Satan manifested himself in the form of an animal that was subtle and sneaky because he knew he didn't have much power. Humankind has always had dominion over the enemy when they allowed God to have authority over them. God could destroy the kingdom of darkness with one word, but He chooses to do it through those who submit to Him.

God designed us to rule! Satan saw what God gave us, and he didn't like it! He wasn't satisfied with being subordinate to something that God created from dirt. Remember, Lucifer was a high-ranking angel, known for his beauty! He was called the son of the morning, thought to have been heaven's worship leader. Now, this once magnificent being is placed under the dominion of something that God made from dirt. How humiliating is that for someone who is so full of pride?! I'm sure it infuriated him. Nevertheless, Satan refused to submit to God's will, so God decided to defeat him through men and women that would choose to submit to His! God wanted man to mirror heaven on earth. He told them to multiply so that the whole earth could be filled with His glory.

Genesis 1:28 (AMP)

28 And God blessed them [granting them certain authority] and said to them, "Be fruitful, multiply, and fill the earth, and subjugate it [putting it under your power]; and rule over (dominate) the fish of the sea, the birds of the air, and every living thing that moves upon the earth."

God told them to dominate, and Satan wasn't about to stand for that. He realized that he didn't have the physical power to wage war on man; he couldn't attack him with actual darts. Therefore, he used the only thing that he could—his words of deception.

Deception is the primary tool Satan uses against us. His attempts to deceive us are designed to take us out of our place of authority. When Adam and Eve were in the garden, Satan had to use manipulation and deception to cheat them out of their dominion.

Genesis 3:3-5 (AMP)

3 Now the serpent was more crafty (subtle, skilled in deceit) than any living creature of the field which the Lord God had made. And the serpent (Satan) said to the woman, "Can it really be that God has said, 'You shall not eat from any tree of the garden'?" 2 And the woman said to the serpent, "We may eat fruit from the trees of the garden, 3 except the fruit from the tree which is in the middle of the garden. God said, 'You shall not eat from it nor touch it, otherwise you will die.'" 4 But the serpent said to the woman, "You certainly will not die! 5 For God knows that on the day you eat from it your eyes will be opened [that is, you will have greater awareness], and you will be like God, knowing [the difference between] good and evil."

God gave them specific instructions, and Satan wanted to twist them to make them doubt God. When they chose to believe his lies, they became unsubmitted and lost their dominion. Remember, you share your authority with whatever you come into agreement with. Adam and Eve gave their authority up because they doubted the word of the Lord. The enemy's tactics have not changed at all. He is still deceiving people into believing the opposite of what God has said. He knows that if he can keep us deceived, he can keep us defeated! However, God saw that man had fallen and was gracious enough to have a plan for redemption!

John 3:16 (AMP)

16 "For God so [greatly] loved and dearly prized the world, that He [even] gave His [One and] only begotten Son, so that whoever believes and trusts in Him [as Savior] shall not perish, but have eternal life.

God's plan to return man's dominion over the influence of darkness surrounded a sacrifice. The blood of bulls and rams could only cover our sins, but the Father desired fellowship with us again. He wanted us to be able to come into His presence freely and walk in the authority He designed us to have, so He sent His Son— Jesus.

The sacrifice that Jesus made on the cross gives every man the opportunity to regain his authority. It ended the separation between God and man, and it put man back on the path to fill the earth with God's glory. Jesus spent a significant amount of time on earth casting out demons. He was confronted by demonic forces everywhere He went. They knew that His presence signified the end of Satan's reign! The glorious manifestation of Jesus on this earth represented the dominion to drive out devils! What angers the entire kingdom of darkness even more is this: when Jesus came, He didn't keep all the power to himself; He shared it with those who chose to believe Him!

Luke 10:19 (AMP)

19 Listen carefully: I have given you authority [that you now possess] to tread on serpents and scorpions, and [the ability to exercise authority] over all the power of the enemy (Satan); and nothing will [in any way] harm you.

In Luke 10, Jesus was teaching His followers the extent of their authority. He taught us that because we choose to believe in him, He has given us authority over ALL the powers of Satan. Jesus was different from every other prophet or man whom God had sent before because He displayed something that had not been seen in the Old Testament days. While we saw healing and miracles in the Old Testament by the Prophets of God, we did not know the ability to cast out devils until Christ came on the scene. Every deliverance minister must remember that our authority comes from Christ! He is the foundation!

Philippians 2:8-11 (AMP)

8 After He was found in [terms of His] outward appearance as a man [for a divinely-appointed time], He humbled Himself [still further] by becoming obedient [to the Father] to the point of death, even death on a cross. 9 For this reason also [because He obeyed and so completely humbled Himself], God has highly exalted Him and bestowed on Him the name which is above every name, 10 so that at the name of Jesus [a]every knee shall bow [in submission], of those who are in heaven and on earth and under the earth, 11 and that every tongue will confess and openly acknowledge that Jesus Christ is Lord (sovereign God), to the glory of God the Father.

Christ had the right to use His authority overall because the Father gave it to Him! Do you notice a pattern here? God gave His *submitted* Son all authority, and Christ gave all authority to His *submitted* followers. The trend is simple—true authority comes through submission. If you have areas in your life where you are oppressed and depressed, they are likely areas in your life that are unsubmitted to the Father. Your submission to God forces the enemy to evacuate your life.

James 4:7 (AMP)
7 So submit to [the authority of] God. Resist the devil [stand firm against him] and he will flee from you.

As a deliverance minister, practicing submission is paramount to your ability to use God's authority. I'm not saying that you have to be perfect and without flaw, but there must be a constant drive from within to submit every part of yourself to God. God isn't looking for instant perfection but steady progression. However, if you have areas in your life where you refuse to submit to the authority of heaven and the word of God, those will be the areas where the enemy resists your authority. Those are also areas the enemy can stand on in order to influence your life. Deliverance is not about a show of authority. We do not become deliverance ministers to prove our anointing or validate our calling. Deliverance ministry is about submitting your heart to God so that you can be a tool for someone else's freedom.

Many years ago, I attended a service where the preacher held an altar call and prophesied to many people. A woman began to manifest demonic spirits, making horse-like noises and walking on all fours. By the look on the preacher's face, it was apparent to everyone that he was terrified. It was a well-known fact that this preacher had unsubmitted areas in his life, particularly as it related to sexual immorality. He began to try and call the spirit under subjection, but the demon wouldn't budge. Instead, it laughed at him and mockingly said "no," continuing its parade. Thankfully, my mother was ready and equipped to cast out the demon successfully. Here's a bit of wisdom from that experience. For years, I assumed that the demon didn't come out of the woman because of the man's sexual sin. I thought that because he wasn't perfect, God wouldn't use him. Meanwhile, as I continued to think on this subject and study, I found that submission was the issue. He did just have a fall. He was unsubmitted to God in the area of his sexuality. That made the enemy laugh. You can only wield the authority to which you yield. Every lease has terms and conditions. The power isn't yours! You're leasing it from Christ, and the terms and conditions are submitting to the counsel of His will!

It is very dangerous to engage in spiritual warfare when you have not fully submitted to the authority of God. God does not look for deliverance ministers to be perfect, but He does expect them to progress. Submission to God is not about works and deeds; submission to God is about your belief systems. When you choose to believe that God's way is the best way and you choose to follow His will above your own, that is submission to God.

Submitting to God and stepping into your position of authority will cause the enemies in your life to manifest themselves. When you truly walk in the light of God's authority, no darkness can hide. Embracing your authority as a believer and an ambassador of heaven sends off alarms in the kingdom of darkness. It tells demons that they have another target to take out before their kingdom is destroyed.

The enemy's plan for your life is to keep you away from your God-given authority. He knows that if he can stop you from coming into agreement with heaven about whom you are and what you're supposed to do, he can influence your life. Many believers sit in church listening to the word of God over and over again and never take the steps toward the submission to God that will enable them to walk in truth! Society teaches us that submission is a sign of weakness, but in God's kingdom, we know that God's strength is made perfect in weakness. It's okay to be weak when the Lord is your strength. Never attempt to cast out any spirit in your own strength because there is no power in your name. You don't have the ability to command the enemy. Remember, your authority is borrowed authority; it belongs to God. You are acting as His representative in the earth realm. When you recognize your authority and operate in it, you will begin to see the glory of God manifest in your life.

When you stand against the enemy, you must stand in authority to command him to leave. It is unnecessary for you to scream, yell, or ask the demon a bunch of questions. You should speak with clarity and confidence and remind your foe whom you represent. There is power in His name! Don't become zealous because demons respond to you. Stay prayerful and vigilant. Inasmuch, keep this in mind: just because something is manifesting doesn't mean it is coming out. If you are at the altar or in a session where manifestations begin to get wild and unruly, you must use your authority to make it stop.

Luke 4:31-35 (AMP)

31 Then He came down [from the hills of Nazareth] to Capernaum, a city of Galilee [on the shore of the sea], and He was teaching them on the Sabbath; 32 and they were surprised [almost overwhelmed] at His teaching, because His message was [given] with authority and power and great ability. 33 There was a man in the synagogue who was possessed by the spirit of an unclean demon; and he cried out with a loud and terrible voice, 34 "Let us alone! [a]What business do we have [in common] with each other, Jesus of Nazareth? Have You come to destroy us? I know who You are—the Holy One of God!" 35 But Jesus rebuked him, saying, "Be silent (muzzled, gagged) and come out of him!" And when the demon had thrown the man down among them, he came out of him without injuring him in any way.

We see in this passage of scripture that a demon manifested because Jesus was teaching with authority! Most times, demons manifest to incite fear or challenge authority. Jesus used his authority and commanded the manifestations to stop and then commanded the demon to come out! We must follow this same practice.

I remember the first time I really started to believe in the authority that we, as believers, have over demonic spirits. As a child, I remember accompanying my mother while she preached during an all-night prayer service. She ministered such a powerful word that people began to testify and confess the things they were dealing with. So much freedom was happening in the room; it was beautiful. One guy stood up to "testify," but soon he started saying foul and horrible things that were just out of the ordinary. My mother immediately discerned that it was a demon in operation, and she addressed it directly. When she did, the man began to shake himself violently. He continued this behavior until my mother sharply commanded him to "stop that." He instantly stood at attention, stiff as a board. I knew it was real because she spoke to him in the same tone in which she spoke to me whenever I acted out as a child. It's funny to think about it that way, but that's the level of boldness you must have.

That day, I embraced the authority that believers have, and I learned to never allow a demon to manifest without speaking directly to it! In the chapters to come, I will teach you how to deal with manifestations in most cases. Demons are unpredictable, but all powers must become subject to the name of Jesus!

Chapter One
Workbook Section

1. Along with an understanding of your spiritual authority, how does your understanding of yourself and life experiences develop you as a deliverance minister? Take 2-3 moments to reflect on the good and bad experiences and write how they have helped/will help you minister to others?

_____

_____

_____

_____

_____

_____

2. Take a moment, and ask yourself: "how much do I trust myself?"

_____

_____

_____

_____

_____

3. After reading this chapter, explain *authority* in your own words.

_____

_____

_____

_____

_____

4. Identify and list the areas in your life that you are not submitted to God.

_____

_____

_____

_____

_____

5. What are places of authority you feel as though you need to regain? (Are these places mental, emotional, physical, etc.?)

_____

_____

_____

_____

6. What areas are you most passionate about seeing people delivered?

_____

_____

_____

    a. The areas that you are most passionate about seeing people delivered are often the areas that you have experienced the most pain.

_____

_____

_____

    b. Are you qualified for deliverance ministry?

_____

_____

_____

Exercise: Write the ways you can leverage your painful experiences to evolve as a powerful deliverance minister.

_____

_____

_____

Chapter Two
Who Are You Fighting?

A smart soldier takes time to gather intel on his opponent before going into battle. We must do the same when engaging in warfare against the enemy. In every deliverance session, you must stay aware that you are warring against a being who is not flesh and blood.

Demons are ancient, intelligent, disembodied spirits. They have personalities! There are many schools of thought concerning the origin of demons. Some believe that they are the angels that fell with Lucifer. Others believe that they are the spirits of a sinful race of people whom God destroyed before Adam. Many believe they are the disembodied spirits of Nephilim, the offspring of angels and humans whom God cursed and destroyed in the flood of Noah. Honestly, their origin isn't that important. It's great information to study, but it can become consuming, kind of like comic books. There are so many different theories and crazy "revelations." The bible isn't explicitly clear on where demons come from. The simple fact is this: they are here; they aim to destroy God's people, and Jesus commissioned us to cast them out in His name!

Demons crave to be in a body so that they can complete their work in the earth realm. There is a major spiritual principle that every spirit including God adheres to. No spirit has legal access to the earth realm. In order for a spirit to have complete access to the earth realm that spirit must be attached to a body. Even God subscribed to this principle when He decided that He wanted the fullness of His deity to walk among men, teach them, and lead them. The difference between the spirit of God and the other spirits is, When God needed a body to do His work among men, He created one! Satan doesn't have that kind of authority. God created Himself a body that was not bound to the sin patterns that came from Adam's loins. He conceived that body in a virgin named Mary. The child's name was called Emmanuel which means "God with us." This is the reason that demons want to connect to humans so desperately! If they can't connect to a human body, they will go into animals to avoid being without a host.

Matthew 8:31-32 (AMP)

31 The demons began begging Him, "If You drive us out, send us into the herd of pigs." 32 And He said to them, "Go!" So they came out [of the men] and went into the pigs, and the whole herd rushed down the steep bank into the sea and died in the water.

Demons have an insatiable drive to influence people into damnation. You must never forget that demons are not all-powerful. They can only do what we allow them to do. When you are born, you are assigned two destinies. One destiny is spoken by out of the mouth of God, and the kingdom of darkness designs the other. When hell assigns you a destiny, it is the complete opposite of what God has said. Because the kingdom of darkness doesn't have creative ability, hell assigns demonic life coaches to every person who is born, and their job is to train you to think in a way that keeps you from your God-spoken destiny!

I know it may be hard to grasp the concept of demons being personalities without bodies, but the scriptures give us many truths about demonic characteristics. Demons have personalities, but they are not human. They do not have a human spirit that can be saved. Listed below are some characteristics of demonic spirits described by Derek Prince with some of my explanations and experiences.

Demons have limited power.
Mark 5:1-18 (AMP)

5 They came to the other side of the sea, to the region of the Gerasenes. 2 When Jesus got out of the boat, immediately a man from the tombs with an unclean spirit met Him, 3 and the man lived in the tombs, and no one could bind him anymore, not even with chains. 4 For he had often been bound with shackles [for the feet] and with chains, and he tore apart the chains and broke the shackles into pieces, and no one was strong enough to subdue and tame him.

They are not all-powerful, but they do have a limited range of power. Demons' ability to affect you solely depends on what you allow them to do. Remember, Christ gave us power over them!

Demons speak.

Acts 19:13-15 (AMP)

13 Then some of the traveling Jewish exorcists also attempted to call the name of the Lord Jesus over those who had evil spirits, saying, "I implore you and solemnly command you by the Jesus whom Paul preaches!" 14 Seven sons of one [named] Sceva, a Jewish chief priest, were doing this. 15 But the evil spirit retorted, "I know and recognize and acknowledge Jesus, and I know about Paul, but as for you, who are you?"

Demons will speak to you when you are casting them out. Remember, they are masters of deception. DO NOT attempt to hold conversations with them or ask them questions. They are liars! Anytime demons spoke in the presence of Jesus, He commanded them to be silent. When you cast out spirits, a demon will speak to declare their rights to the person's soul. They will threaten you, and they will even mock or attempt to taunt you. Never lose your focus. Command them to come out!

Demons have feelings.

Matthew 8:29 (AMP)

29 And they screamed out, "[a]What business do we have [in common] with each other, Son of God? Have You come to torment us before the appointed time [of judgment]?"

In this scripture, we see the emotions that demons feel about leaving a person's life. It is torment for them to be cast out. There have been many times in sessions when demons would beg me not to cast them out. Every spirit has its own personality. Some spirits show anger about having to come out. On some occasions, I have had demons cry and beg not to be cast out. I've been in services where demons tried to run from me in fear of being cast out! You must never show sympathy to any demon. It is your job to call them out, so the person can be set free because demons are NOT your friends.

Demons have knowledge.

Acts 16:16-18 (AMP)

16 It happened that as we were on our way to the place of prayer, we were met by a slave-girl who had a spirit of divination [that is, a demonic spirit claiming to foretell the future and discover hidden knowledge], and she brought her owners a good profit by fortune-telling. 17 She followed after Paul and us and kept screaming and shouting, "These men are servants of the Most High God! They are proclaiming to you the way of salvation!" 18 She continued doing this for several days. Then Paul, being greatly annoyed and worn out, turned and said to the spirit [inside her], "I command you in the name of Jesus Christ [as His representative] to come out of her!" And it came out at that very moment.

This spirit that followed Paul was speaking the truth, but it still had to come out. Never listen to the intelligence from demons. Another tool in the enemy's arsenal is flattery! Don't be deceived;

stay connected to what the Holy Spirit is saying! Flattery is an open door to deception and torment. Demons are not all-knowing, but the demonic realm has an intricate surveillance network. They are always attempting to watch and listen to gather intel against the children of God. This is one reason that Satan is called the accuser! Actually, the word *Satan* in Hebrew literally means accuser! It's not just whom he is, but it's what he does. Demons want to seem all-knowing to intimidate us, but they are not. The book of Isaiah talks about spirits who peep and mutter to mediums and necromancers. When you are submitted to God, you are hidden under the shadow of His mighty power. No spirit can peep into your life.

Demons have a will and desires.

Matthew 12:43-45 (AMP)
43 "Now when the unclean spirit has gone out of a man, it roams through waterless (dry, arid) places in search of rest, but it does not find it. 44 Then it says, 'I will return to my house from which I came.' And when it arrives, it finds the place unoccupied, swept, and put in order. 45 Then it goes and brings with it seven other spirits more wicked than itself, and they go in and make their home there. And the last condition of that man becomes worse than the first. So will it also be with this wicked generation.

All demons desire to have a home, but some demons will try to live out their desires and personalities through the person whom they suppress or oppress. Demons will let you know their desires.

19

When you begin to command them to come out of a person, sometimes they will declare their will. I once cast a demon out of a woman, and a demon spoke through her to say, "I will not go. I must have her children."

Demons have community.

Luke 4:34 (AMP)

34 "Let us alone! What business do we have [in common] with each other, Jesus of Nazareth? Have You come to destroy us? I know who You are—the Holy One of God!"

Demons gather together like flies on a dead carcass. You will never find one demon oppressing someone alone. They always bring their friends along to the party. When casting them out, it is good to study and find out which demons like to hang out with each other. Demons protect each other. Just like there are rankings and order in our military, there is ranking in the kingdom of darkness; the strongest demons are usually the last to come out.

You can find these characteristics repeated in the scriptures. The concepts of demons are in cultures all over the world. Although the names vary, the traits are the same. Demons are evil, and they come to torment. Don't allow yourself to become fascinated with studying demonology. It can make you become an extremist, and you will start thinking that everything that you run into is a demon. We do not live-in reaction to darkness; we must live in response to God's word!

Chapter Two
Workbook Section

1. What does Mark 16:17 teach us about believers?

   _____

   _____

   _____

   _____

   _____

2. Define the *Kingdom of God.*

   _____

   _____

   _____

   _____

   _____

3. What has been the consistent thing of deception in your life?
   Examples: worth, identity, acceptance, ability.

   _____

   _____

   _____

Exercise: As stated in this chapter, demons are masters of deception. Write down ways you have seen the enemy deceive you and your perspective.

_____

_____

_____

_____

_____

Exercise: Now that you know the truth about the enemy's authority and how dependent he is on you, write him a letter evicting him from your mind, will, and emotions. Afterwards, take time to read it out loud.

_____

_____

_____

_____

_____

_____

Chapter Three
Signs of Demonic Influence

Demons manifest in the lives of people in many different ways. Their objective is to stay hidden so that they can complete their work. They are the source for many cases of mental trauma, physical pain, and emotional health issues. I have seen many healings and miracles through the ministry of deliverance because when the root is cut out, the fruit has to dry up! Recognizing demonic influence is a powerful skill that every believer should develop.

The enemy is masterful in the art of deception, so the discerning of spirits is a gift that you need to ask God to give you! I'm not talking about discernment or suspicion. I'm talking about the authentic gift of God that is rooted in love. Suspicion tries to come to conclusion through carnal senses and memories. The true gift of discerning of spirits gets to the root of the matter quickly and doesn't hesitate to show the love needed to set someone free! Suspicion judges the person. Discerning of spirits judges the enemy of that person's soul!

I was casting demons out of a lady when the Lord showed me that she had a tumor on her brain. I asked her about it, and she confirmed that she'd received the same diagnosis from her doctor. At the end of her session, I told her to go to the doctor and see if he/she could find the tumor. I am confident that by the power of deliverance, she has been healed completely.

On another occasion, I had a young man who could not sleep at all. A demon of insomnia had come upon him. The doctors had prescribed medication to help him sleep, but nothing was working. The Lord told me to have him bring one of his pillows from his bed, so I could pray over it. I prayed over the pillow, turned to him, and commanded the spirit of insomnia to leave him. He gave a massive yawn, and I knew that he would never have that issue again. He called me the next day and told me that he had the best sleep of his life that night!

There are many signs of demonic influence. Remember, demons are ancient intelligent personalities, so it is dangerous to box them into one definition. The manifestation listed below are just some of the most common ways to identify demonic influence.

Oppression

Mark 9:20-23 (AMP)

20 They brought the boy to Him. When the [demonic] spirit saw Him, immediately it threw the boy into a convulsion, and falling to the ground he began rolling around and foaming at the mouth. 21 Jesus asked his father, "How long has this been happening to him?" And he answered, "Since childhood. 22 The demon has often thrown him both into fire and into water, intending to kill him. But if You can do anything, take pity on us and help us!" 23 Jesus said to him, "[You say to Me,] 'If You can?' All things are possible for the one who believes and trusts [in Me]!"

In this scripture, we see an example of oppression. The boy's father told Jesus that the demon who had influence over the child would compel him to commit suicidal acts. Any time a person is experiencing any type of oppression, there is a demonic spirit at work. Oppression doesn't have to bring the person any pleasure at all. If there is something that he/she wants to stop doing and can't, it should be dealt with through deliverance. Oppression manifests in many compulsive disorders: shopping, hoarding, eating, gambling, sex, exercise, etc. When a person is dealing with oppression, he/she is trapped in a pattern of repetitive and senseless thinking. These thought processes can prove difficult to overcome without the ministry of deliverance followed by therapy to help retrain thought life.

Sin Cycles

Romans 6:16 (AMP)

16 Do you not know that when you continually offer yourselves to someone to do his will, you are the slaves of the one whom you obey, either [slaves] of sin, which leads to death, or of obedience, which leads to righteousness (right standing with God)?

We were all born into sin because of Adam and Eve's mistakes. To sin means to miss the mark or to trespass, but the type of sin that causes enslavement is bigger than just missing the mark. Sin cycles are categorized as iniquity. Iniquity is when you know that what you are doing is sin, but you won't or can't stop it.

Iniquity and sin cycles can be inherited from your parents and cause generational bondage. For example, my ancestors practiced divination and witchcraft. I was never taught any witchcraft, but as a child, I had an unhealthy interest in things of the occult. It was because that iniquity was tied to my bloodline.

Many Christians confess their belief in Jesus Christ and strive to follow Him, but they are still enslaved to sin cycles. When Christ died on the cross, He eliminated the power that sin had over us. Any time you find a believer who has fasted, prayed, and cried out to God but can't seem to be separated from a particular sin, you will find a demon at work. There is an open door to his/her soul that has to be shut. They must allow the Lordship of Christ to reign in that area. Many times, people stay in sin cycles because of shame. God wants His people to be free. Your job as a deliverance minister is to make sure that the person you are praying for feels free of shame so that they can confess and be healed. The person must confess their sin and confess that Jesus is Lord.

Addiction

Proverbs 25:28 (KJV)
28 He that hath no rule over his own spirit is like a city that is broken down, and without walls.

When you combine oppression and sin cycles, you get an addiction. I have seen many types of addictions during my time as a deliverance minister. Any form of addiction is tied to very strong demonic influence. The *American Heritage Dictionary* describes *addiction* as a compulsive physical or mental need for habit-forming substances, activities, or experiences. Addiction is also characterized by a behavior performed in response to an obsession. Here is a list of common addictions that can be broken through the power of deliverance:

1. Substance: alcohol, heroin, tobacco, solvents, cocaine, crack, cannabis, caffeine, steroids, tranquilizers, hallucinogens, amphetamines, ecstasy, painkillers, barbiturates, etc.

2. Social: overexercising, sex, sexual perversions, pornography, eating disorders (anorexia, bulimia, overeating), techno-addictions (computer games, cybersex), work, gambling, etc.

Mental Torment

Matthew 18:34-35 (AMP)

34 And in wrath his master turned him over to the torturers (jailers) until he paid all that he owed. 35 My heavenly Father will also do the same to [every one of] you, if each of you does not forgive his brother from your heart."

One of the most common signs of demonic influence is mental torment. One of the major open doors to mental torment is unforgiveness. In the scripture above, Christ teaches us about a person who was turned over to tormentors because he refused to forgive.

I define *mental torment* as a lack of peace. People who are constantly afraid, worried, angry, anxious, or sad are people who likely have come under some form of demonic oppression. God's word tells us how to think and overcome mental warfare, but when we don't submit to that word, we open ourselves up to attack.

I once prayed for a woman of God who had severe knee pain. During the interview portion of our deliverance session, I found out that she constantly worried about her son. That mental torment manifested in her body, and the only way she experienced any type of release was through pain medication. We prayed forgiveness prayers; she released worry, and I commanded pain to leave her. Two years later, I went back to her church. She testified that she never had to use medication again. She was completely healed!

Mental torment includes, but is not limited to, hearing voices, fears and phobias, suicidal tendencies, anger and violence, self-condemnation, and depression. Fear can also manifest as dark shadows following you.

Demonic influence is not the same as demonic possession. Possession is a poor translation. The original wording in the scripture for possession should have been translated as demonized. The KJV incorrectly translates it to be "possessed with devils." There is nothing in the original Greek to support the word *possessed*, which is completely misleading. Possession suggests ownership, and we cannot be owned by demons. However, Christians with unsubmitted areas in their heart can be influenced and oppressed by the kingdom of darkness. Deliverance ministry is a needed part of every person's life.

Trauma

Isaiah 41:10 (KJV)

10 Fear thou not; for I am with thee: be not dismayed; for I am thy God: I will strengthen thee; yea, I will help thee; yea, I will uphold thee with the right hand of my righteousness.

The final common sign of demonic influence that I'd like to elaborate on is unaddressed trauma. Traumatic experiences happen to many people every day. They can be physical, mental, and emotional. Trauma affects each person differently and can manifest itself in a person's soul in a number of ways. Trauma often needs to be addressed by a seasoned deliverance minister and a therapist. I've seen the effects of trauma show up in small ways, like how someone responds to a raised voice, but I've also seen some major manifestations of trauma like the creations of other identities. Some people have these life-altering experiences at a very early age, and the aftereffect can be devastating. The enemy wants to use the effects of this event to keep a person paralyzed at the point of his/her past trauma. Trauma is venomous and causes gifted believers to be stuck in the past. The enemy works to magnify trauma. Demons use traumatic events to keep a person from developing into what God designed him/her to be.

Chapter Three
Workbook Section

1. How does your discernment work? In what ways does the Holy Spirit alert you to demonic activity?

_____

_____

_____

_____

_____

2. Is there any unhealthy compulsive activity in your life that has led you into places of oppression? When did these start?

_____

_____

_____

_____

_____

3. If fortunate to administer deliverance, what are some ways you can ensure you are conveying the ministry of love?

_____

_____

_____

_____

_____

Exercise: Sit with the Holy Spirit and ask how unforgiveness manifested into mental, emotional, or physical torment. Write down what He says.

_____

_____

_____

_____

_____

_____

_____

_____

_____

Chapter Four
The Development of Strongholds

We are at war, and if you aren't fighting, you've already been captured. The battleground where the enemy attacks is in the mind! Remember, Satan doesn't have any physical power! His only power is deception, and after thousands of years, his tactics have not changed. He attacks by creating strongholds. Hell is desperate to influence the thought life of every human being on this planet because if darkness can affect your mind, darkness can shape your world.

Adam and Eve were living in paradise and were given the mandate to be heaven's ambassadors on the earth. God breathed His breath into Adam and formed Eve with His own hands, but Satan was still able to deceive them by influencing Eve's thoughts about what God said. When Eve came into agreement with the lies of Satan, she legally turned over her authority to him. Like Eve, you share authority with whatever you come into agreement with. Christ has since come and restored dominion back to those who choose to serve Him, but authority can still be stolen through agreement. What lies about yourself have you agreed with? What has your authority?

Because the battleground for spiritual warfare is the mind, the kingdom of darkness will throw thoughts, ideas, and concepts into your mind to gain agreement in your thought life. As a believer, the enemy should not be given any ground in your mind because he has no legal right to your thought life. Your mind should be an environment where fear, doubt, discouragement, and any other attack from the enemy can't breathe! Satan is a legalist which means that for him to take a space, he must have an agreement with the person who owns it. You are in charge of your own mental space. Therefore, every time you believe the enemy's perspective about yourself and your destiny, you sign an agreement for Satan to have space in your mind. He endeavors to gain influence in your life so that you'll become bound by his perspective. Once Satan starts leasing space in your mind, he starts building a stronghold. The particular type of stronghold the enemy specializes in are those that are control towers, not fortresses. A fortress is a place of solitude and safety; thus, God is a fortress. Whereas, a stronghold is a place of bondage and contempt.

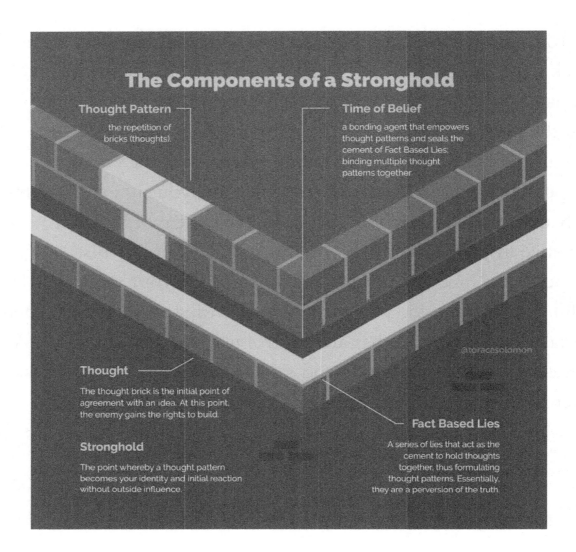

The Components of a Stronghold

Thought Pattern
the repetition of bricks (thoughts).

Time of Belief
a bonding agent that empowers thought patterns and seals the cement of Fact Based Lies; binding multiple thought patterns together

Thought
The thought brick is the initial point of agreement with an idea. At this point, the enemy gains the rights to build.

Stronghold
The point whereby a thought pattern becomes your identity and initial reaction without outside influence.

Fact Based Lies
A series of lies that act as the cement to hold thoughts together, thus formulating thought patterns. Essentially, they are a perversion of the truth.

@toracesolomon

strong·hold

a place where a particular perspective or belief is strongly defended or upheld; they are mentalities used to manifest unseen assignments into reality!

Strongholds are:

1. Defended and Hidden
2. Industrial and Residential Mental Property
3. Demonic Control Towers
4. Can Only Be Built on Legal Ground

The way Satan asserts his influence is by seducing you to create mentalities, perspective, and ideologies that oppose the will of God for your life. Strongholds are built to defend the ground demons win by gaining your agreement. Demons need human agreement to do their work.

We've been taught that strongholds are spiritual structures and that we can pull them down with physical gestures. That's cute, but the truth is that every spiritual stronghold is rooted in thought. That's the way Satan attacks! You have to quickly identify the ideas and thoughts planted by evil spirits because believing one thought from darkness will duplicate and lead you to negative thought patterns. Thoughts become thought patterns, and thought patterns become strongholds once your belief empowers them.

The construction of strongholds starts in our conscious mind. Remember the battleground for warfare is the mind, and any good warrior surveys the battlefield before the fight. Let's take a look at how the mind works. According to Sigmund Freud's psychoanalytic theory of personality, the conscious mind consists of everything inside of our current awareness. This means the conscious mind is involved with things we are actively thinking about. For example, right now, you are using your conscious mind to read this book and digest the information. The conscious mind is active when you are learning new information like trying out a new recipe.

Demonic influence begins in the conscious mind but doesn't stay there. As soon as we grab hold of the seductive information the enemy presents to our conscious mind, he starts working overtime to create thought patterns. Demonic influence creates thought patterns by connecting a conscious thought with a preconscious memory. Preconscious thoughts are things that are not in our current thinking but can easily be brought into conscious awareness. For example, you may not be actively thinking about your address, but it can easily be brought into recollection when needed. In the case of deliverance, the enemy creates thought patterns by connecting our preconscious thinking about mistakes, offenses, and traumas of the past with the current perspective he is presenting to our conscious mind.

Here's a scenario to explain the creation of strongholds. You experience a bad breakup with someone you were really invested in. The enemy tries to take advantage of that situation by presenting a thought like " I'm alone" into your conscious thinking. At that point, you will immediately be reminded of the pain of other failed relationships. The glue that connects the conscious thought and the preconscious thought is fact-based lies. Fact-based lies are the details from the past thinking and current thinking that seem to match up and align. In this scenario, the facts are correct because you did have more than one failed relationship, but the conclusion from these facts are not true! The facts say you haven't had good luck with relationships, but the truth according to God's word is that you will never be alone. The conscious thoughts and the preconscious thoughts that are held together by fact-based lies work in repetition to create thought patterns. The thought is " I'm alone," but the thought pattern is " I'll always be alone." Thought patterns easily slip from the conscious mind to the subconscious mind. It's important to note that the enemy will suggest thoughts in the first person so that you will take ownership of these thoughts more easily. Every thought that begins with "I" isn't yours.

The subconscious mind is the autopilot part of the thinking. I believe that 90 percent of the things that we do are not a part of our conscious thinking; it is the work of our mind on autopilot. For example, you start a new job, and for the first few days, you have to actively think (i.e. your conscious mind) about your route to work. After a couple of weeks of taking the same route to work every day, your subconscious takes over, and you don't have to actively think about your route. Negative thought patterns in the conscious mind are built using this same regiment. You have to detox your mind from the enemy's automation because if negative thought patterns sit in the subconscious mind long enough and we react to the world from that place long enough it becomes a stronghold and a part of our identity.

Progression of Strongholds

Stage	Definition	Example	Area
Thought	The initial idea, concept perspective or imagination	"I can't do this."	Conscious
Thought Pattern	A habit of thinking in a particular way, using particular assumptions	"I can't do this. Things never work out for me."	Subconscious
Stronghold	A strongly defended mentality that comes from a consistent way of thinking.	"I'm a failure."	Conscience

Deliverance ministry is about influence! Demons oppress people so that they can have their influence and take their lives! The kingdom of darkness knows that God has given us dominion. Demons also know that the power of life and death is in our tongue. Demons don't have the creative and destructive power that God put in our mouths, so they attempt to take it by launching these mental attacks and creating strongholds. According to Isaiah 14, his desire was to ascend and build his kingdom (strongholds) ABOVE (exalted higher than) the kingdom of God. Consequently, he was knocked down, and since then, he's consistently been held to the low place God sent him to.

It is important to note the following:

1. He couldn't build his kingdom in heaven because God has dominion there!
2. He couldn't build his kingdom on earth because God gave dominion to man!
3. Now, the only place he can build his kingdom is the mind of men who give him the right!

Proverbs 18:21 (AMP)

21 Death and life are in the power of the tongue, And those who love it and indulge it will eat its fruit and bear the consequences of their words.

Demons go to the source of all of our speech, which is the mind. Every word of life or death that you speak from your mouth starts in your mind. If the demonic can influence your mind, it can influence your words. Inasmuch, if the demonic can influence your words, it can shape your world. The kingdom of darkness wants your world to be dark and miserable. Demons want to keep you away from the power of Christ so that they can destroy your life! They are actively trying to plant thoughts in your head about everything. They want your perspective to be perverted because they know that your fulfilled destiny is intended to be a fountain of life for many!

God's word is the only way to fortify your mind and break down strongholds. Studying what the bible says about your identity as a Christian is your primary defense against the demonic realm. If you do not understand your authority, you will fail to defend yourself against the demonic. For example, demons tell people that they have no destiny and no purpose, and they will never find happiness. In deliverance, you must directly confront these lies with biblical truths! Wholly believing in these truths is the first step to regaining ground in your mind and breaking down strongholds.

After you identify the lies of Satan and confront them with the truth, the next step is to evict the strongman. When the demonic is allowed to build strongholds in your mind, they don't leave them empty. Every stronghold houses a strong man (a demon). For you to regain that ground mentally, you must cast out the demon from that stronghold by the authority of Christ. The strong man's job is to influence your life from the inside. Remember strongholds are residential and industrial property. What this means is demons work out of strongholds to manipulate your life and spread their influence. It's like a factory, so not only is it a place where demons live, but strongholds are places where demons gather in groups to live and work. Demons are never alone. The strongman is the leader of the stronghold. He invites other demons in to reinforce this negative fortress and help it spread into other areas. When in deliverance, it's important for you to understand the types of demons that often work together. This is important to understand when moving in deliverance ministry because demons try to hide. When calling out the strongman demon, make sure you call out every spirit associated with them.

Here is a list of common demon groupings.

Strongman	Common Partners	Strongman	Common Partners
ACCUSATION	Judging, Criticism, Fault-Finding	ADDICTION	Nicotine, Alcohol, Drugs, Medications, Caffeine, Gluttony
AFFECTATION	Theatrics, Playacting, Sophistication, Pretension	BITTERNESS	Violence, Temper, Anger, Resentment, Hatred, Unforgiveness, Retaliation, Murder
CONFUSION	Frustration, Incoherence, Forgetfulness, Circular Reasoning	COMPETITION	Driving, Argument, Pride, Ego
CONTROL	Possessiveness, Dominance, Witchcraft	COVETOUSNESS	Stealing, Kleptomania, Material, Lust, Greed, Discontent
CURSING	Blasphemy, Coarse, Jesting, Gossip, Criticism, Backbiting, Mockery, Belittling, Railing	DEPRESSION	Despair, Despondency, Discouragement, Defeatism, Dejection, Suicide, Hopelessness, Death, Insomnia, Morbidity
DOUBT	Unbelief, Skepticism	ESCAPE	Indifference, Stoicism, Passivity, Sleepiness, Alcohol, Drugs
FALSE BURDEN	False responsibility, False compassion, Fatigue, Tiredness, Weariness, Laziness	FEARS	Fear of death, Fear of rejection, Fear of failure, Fear of success, Fear of the future, Fear of abandonment, Fear of loneliness

Phobias (all kinds) Hysteria	Arachnophobia, Acrophobia, Agoraphobia, Cynophobia, Astraphobia, Trypanophobia, Social Phobias, Mysophobia	**GRIEF**	Crying, Sadness, Cruel, Sorrow, Heartache, Heartbreak
GUILT	Condemnation, Unworthiness, Embarrassment	**GLUTTONY**	Nervousness, Compulsive, Eating, Resentment, Frustration, Idleness, Self-pity, Self-reward
HEAVINESS	Burden, Gloom, Disgust	**HYPERACTIVITY**	Restlessness, Driving, Pressure
INDECISION	Procrastination, Compromise, Confusion, Forgetfulness, Indifference	**INHERITANCE**	Physical, Emotional, Mental, Curses
IMPATIENCE	Agitation, Frustration, Intolerance, Resentment, Criticism	**MIND-BINDING**	Confusion, Fear of man, Fear of failure, Occult Spirits, Spiritism Spirits
INFIRMITY	May include any sickness or disease	**INSECURITY**	Inferiority, Self-pity, Loneliness, Timidity, Shyness, Inadequacy, Ineptness
JEALOUSY	Envy, Distrust, Suspicion, Selfishness	**MENTAL ILLNESS**	Insanity, Madness, Mania, Senility, Schizophrenia, Paranoia, Hallucinations
MIND IDOLATRY	Intellectualism, Rationalization, Pride, Ego Humanism	**NERVOUSNESS**	Tension, Headache, Nervous habits, Restlessness, Excitement, Insomnia, Roving, Striving

PARANOIA	Jealousy, Envy, Suspicion, Distrust, Fears, Persecution, Confrontation	**PASSIVITY**	Funk, Indifference, Listlessness, Lethargy
PERFECTION	Pride, Vanity, Ego, Frustration, Criticism, Irritability, Intolerance, Anger	**PERSECUTION**	Unfairness, Fear of judgement, Fear of condemnation, Fear of accusation, Fear of reproof, Sensitivity
PRIDE	Ego, Vanity, Self-righteousness, Haughtiness, Importance, Arrogance	**REBELLION**	Self-will, Stubbornness, Disobedience, Anti-submissiveness
RELIGIOSITY	Legalism, Rigidity, Self-righteousness, Judgement, Condemnation	**REJECTION**	Self-rejection
RETALIATION	Destruction, Spite, Hatred, Sadism, Hurt, Cruelty	**SELF-ACCUSATION**	Self-hatred, Self-condemnation
SELF-DECEPTION	Self-delusion, Self-seduction, Pride	**SENSITIVITY**	Self-awareness, Fear of man, Fear of disapproval
STRIFE	Contention, Bickering, Argument, Quarreling, Fighting	**VICTIM**	Self-pity, Bitterness, Entitlement, Embellishment
WITHDRAWAL	Pouting, Daydreaming, Fantasy, Pretension, Unreality	**WORRY**	Anxiety, Fear, Dread, Apprehension

Demonic forces have the power to influence anyone who will listen, including Christians.

Matthew 16:23 (AMP)

23 But Jesus turned and said to Peter, "Get behind Me, Satan! You are a stumbling block to Me; for you are not setting your mind on things of God, but on things of man."

Peter, under the influence of Satan, rebelled against God's plan to redeem us through Jesus' death. Peter gave space for that influence because he wouldn't submit to the word that Jesus spoke. Think about that. Peter was a part of Christ's inner circle. He was the one who walked on water with Christ. He was one of the ones to whom Christ gave authority. He was one of the ones onto whom Christ breathed the Holy Spirit, but the moment he refused to submit to God's word, he was influenced by the demonic.

Luke 22:3-4 (AMP)

3 Then Satan entered Judas, the one called Iscariot, who was one of the twelve [disciples]. 4 And he went away and discussed with the chief priests and officers how he might betray Him and hand Him over to them.

Satan influenced Judas to betray Christ. Peter and Judas were men who walked with Christ daily. They witnessed his miracles and sat directly under his teachings, but they were still influenced by the deceptive nature of the demonic realm. Am I saying that they were possessed? No! What I am saying is: if there are undecided spaces in your mind, the enemy can attack you from those spaces. Possession is a definite term that suggests complete control. Any demon's goal is possession, but as a Christian, you have the tools to fight it. If you have received the Holy Spirit, you must allow nothing except Him to influence you!

Ephesians 6:17 teaches us how to defend our minds against demonic warfare— we do so by putting on the helmet of salvation. This is the portion of the armor of God that guards the mind. Paul mentioned the helmet of salvation again in his first letter to the Thessalonians with a little more detail.

1 Thessalonians 5:8 (NASB)

8 But since we are of the day, let us be [a]sober, having put on the breastplate of faith and love, and as a helmet, the hope of salvation.

Here Paul calls the helmet "the hope of salvation." The protection for your mind against demonic warfare is the hope of salvation. In the original Greek, "hope of salvation" can be translated in a few different ways. Hope is translated as expectation, but the word *salvation* can also be translated as deliverance. Paul is teaching us that the protection we need for our mind is in positive thinking. The expectation of God's faithfulness to set us free blocks out the darkness that the demonic realm wants to place in our minds.

The Enemies of Negative Strongholds

1. **The Word**- Jeremiah says that God's word is like a hammer. The truth, positivity, and identity that we find in the word of

God will break every demonic structure in our thinking.

2. **The Truth**- Since strongholds are built upon agreement with lies, the best way to dismantle them is with the truth.

3. **Positivity**- Strongholds are designed to make you look at life from a negative perspective. They are the control tower for demonic activity in the lives of people.

Continually expecting the preservation of the Lord in every situation will shield your mind from every demonic attack. Positive thinking is a powerful spiritual defense that you must master as a deliverance minister. You cannot be effective with a weak mind. If you are thrown off by every negative situation that comes against you, deliverance ministry is not a place where you should expect to thrive.

Paul gave us another beautiful lesson in spiritual warfare in his letter to the gifted church at Corinth.

2 Corinthians 10:5 (NKJV)

5 casting down arguments and every high thing that exalts itself against the knowledge of God, bringing every thought into captivity to the obedience of Christ,

The first point that we must pull out of this verse is that mental attacks never stop. When you genuinely stand for God and the ministry of deliverance, casting down arguments will become second nature to you. The term *casting down* is a powerful term that suggests that we should be aggressive about dismantling the lies of the enemy in our lives and the lives of others. The reason the enemy has a desire to make strongholds high (exalted) is for one reason: **he wants to be worshipped and seen.**

In the original Greek for this verse, the word *knowledge* is translated as wisdom, meaning the lies from the demonic are designed to oppose all things that come from God's wisdom. They block revelation, strategy, creativity, and inspiration. The wisdom of God is the key to life and growth, so we have to be quick to identify the thoughts that are planted from hell to ensure that the flow of God's wisdom is never hindered.

The last part of this verse shows us that the way to keep the attacks of the enemy from having an effect is by making our thoughts captive to the obedience of Christ! Jesus' obedience and submission to His Father allowed Him to do the impossible, which is what God wants for you also! However, you must follow His Son's obedience. Christ showed us how to bring heaven's power into the earth by living a submitted life. The obedience of Christ is clarified in two passages of scripture.

John 5:19 (NASB)
19 Therefore Jesus answered and was saying to them, "Truly, truly, I say to you, the Son can do nothing of Himself, unless it is something He sees the Father doing; for whatever the Father does, these things the Son also does in like manner.

John 8:28 (NASB)
28 So Jesus said, "When you lift up the Son of Man, then you will know that

I am He, and I do nothing on My own initiative, but I speak these things as the Father taught Me.

Jesus trusted in His Father so much that His eyes and ears were entirely attuned to what God said and did—He was completely obedient. In that same way, every deliverance minister must be completely compliant to win the war against Satan. Jesus fixed His eyes and ears to the frequency of heaven because He knew that what we see and hear directly affects our thought life. It is extremely important for you to make sure that you are only surrounded by the positive and Godly. Don't watch or listen to anyone or anything that would take your focus away from your assignment to operate by the finger of God.

I'm going to give you an easy way to identify thoughts from hell. The bible teaches us how to think, and if we practice this next verse, we can quickly identify thoughts planted by the demonic.

Philippians 4:8 (AMP)

8 Finally, believers, whatever is true, whatever is honorable and worthy of respect, whatever is right and confirmed by God's word, whatever is pure and wholesome, whatever is lovely and brings peace, whatever is admirable and of good repute; if there is any excellence, if there is anything worthy of praise, think continually on these things [center your mind on them, and implant them in your heart].

If a thought comes to your mind that doesn't resemble anything listed in the above passage of scripture, examine it. All of these things listed here are positive. Demons will never bring positive thoughts to your mind because they want you to be discouraged. They know that God does not use discouraged people. You can overcome all the attacks of hell by staying positive and full of courage!

Chapter Four
Workbook Section

1. Are you thinking negative thoughts before you fall asleep?

_____

_____

_____

_____

2. Are you employing a healthy perspective?

_____

_____

_____

_____

_____

3. What limiting beliefs impact your life in undesirable ways? What is the origin of each belief? Is each belief still true for you today? What positive beliefs would counterbalance each one?

_____

_____

_____

_____

4. Have you ever been angry with God? If so, when, and why?

_____

_____

_____

_____

_____

_____

_____

_____

_____

_____

5. The book states that Satan is a legalist. Explain what does being legalistic mean?

_____

_____

_____

_____

_____

_____

Exercise: Identify your most powerful stronghold. Partner with the Holy Spirit and search for the initial thought.

_____

_____

_____

_____

_____

_____

Exercise: After you have identified the initial thought that led to a stronghold, write down how the initial thought progressed into affecting your identity. Explain what the initial thought was, and then explain the thought pattern and how it has affected you as a stronghold.

_____

_____

_____

_____

_____

_____

_____

_____

_____

_____

_____

_____

_____

_____

Chapter 5
Generational Curses

When observing the enemy's tactics against humanity, we have to take a look at a bigger narrative. Embracing the bigger picture can be hard for the immature because we are skilled at identifying the plan of the enemy for our personal lives only! We usually are aware of our own pain and discomfort and deal with it through various unhealthy means. We continuously focus on the war for our soul, never considering the pain that everyone in our bloodline could be in! Isolation is a powerful tactic of the kingdom of darkness. The demonic realm wants you to be consumed with your problems so that you will be blind to the attack against your family. The assignment against you individually is just a microcosm of the assignment of hell against your family! Every family has a mandate from heaven, and because of that mandate, every family has to fight against hell! Families are the most potent representation of God's kingdom! This is why Satan takes so much pleasure in seeing destruction woven into our bloodline through generational curses. Generational curses are not spirits, but they are a contract that the enemy uses to gain access to a family to destroy their purpose legally.

Generational curses alienate a family structure from God's presence and separate them from the benefit of being a part of God's family. We see examples of this when we look at the very first curse that came upon humankind: the curse of sin. When God created Adam, He created him to live a long life of peace and prosperity. He was given divine favor and dominion over the whole earth, but that ended when he allowed the sin of disobedience to enter his life. Because of his sin, everyone born from his loins carried the curse of sin and death. Sin passed on from generation to generation! As time went on, a pattern formed. Sin began taking on different forms and kept transferring from parent to child! Jesus came to destroy the power of sin, but the pattern goes on in those who don't accept Him as Lord!

You have to understand why the attack against families is so strong. Anytime God chose to release a new thing into the earth realm He chose a family. New covenants were given to families. Blessings were released to families! Healthy families are the natural representation of God's glory in the earth! It's about legacy which is why the foundation of every family is attacked with the most weight. The foundation of every family is the mother and the father, but the attack starts when they are sons and daughters. Don't play checkers when a generational curse that's playing chess!

The framework for parents, according to the biblical model, is the Father and the Mother. The attack on these two individuals is duplicated and magnified in their children! The good, the bad, and the ugly impact the family for generations to come! We have to understand the enemy's tool of legalism! When someone in your bloodline makes dysfunction a habit, it's passed down through two channels: nurture or nature. Generational curses are fastened to a person's life by the environment a person was raised in or by his/her DNA or prenatal disposition.

The enemy does not have the authority to come into our lives on his own. Therefore, he creates loopholes and agreements that grant him access to us. I like to call generational curses that are passed down by the environment a person developed in nurture generational curses. These types of generational curses have everything to do with how you are raised. The environment you grow in directly affects your behavior and perspectives as an adult! When our experiences modify the way we interact with our environment, it's called behavioral development. The enemy wants to influence the way we behave as soon as possible. When uncovering the way he attacks, we must take time to look at early development! This process begins in the womb and continues into old age. Multiple environmental factors influence nurture generational curses, including but not limited to, the parents raising and development, educational and economic achievements, mental health and physical health and spiritual health.

Nurture generational curses manifest in us because we are trained to amplify some of the same perspectives that our parents have. It is easy for us to be parented into dysfunctional family traditions and superstitions that give the enemy the green light that he needs to start building mentalities and strongholds in our lives. For example, a generational curse of abuse can be over a family! Let's say a child witnesses his/her mother being abused by his/her father for his/her whole life. That environment nurtures several different perspectives. Many are different fruit from the same cursed roots. The child could grow up full of hatred and anger because of what he/she saw done to his/her mother. That environment grants access to negative spiritual powers!

On the other hand, that same environment can also breed fear, intimidation, and timidity. Two children can be raised in the same environment and develop two opposite responses to their parenting. This assignment on a person's life is directly connected to his/her destiny and the destiny of his/her children. Generational curses aren't carbon copy contracts; they are designed to advance their impact with every generation. Generational curses evolve and work hard to keep the root hidden! They want to open the door for as much demonic influence as possible! That's why the attack on the way we are nurtured is so great. Parents must be aware of this when raising children. Nurture generational curses can travel through the words and actions of parents, grandparents, aunts, uncles, cousins, or anyone trusted to be a part of the village that raises a child. Be careful whom you give space to speak into a child's life. The attack starts in your early development! Parents and guardians are responsible for helping a child evolve into a healthy member of the kingdom of God, but when negative environments are perpetuated the child will have to retrain his/her mind and war for the proper perspective as an adult.

The second way that generational curses latch onto a life is through nature generational curses. Nurture and nature are two very different approaches that the enemy uses to gain access to our bloodline. While nurture is the influence of external factors after conception like parenting, life experiences, and environment, nature is our prenatal wiring and is influenced by genetic inheritance and biological factors like blood! Generational curses that are bound to a person by nature deals with the agreement that a spirit may have with your bloodline. You can be raised in a completely safe environment, but if there is a contract with your blood, you will be enticed by the spirits associated with that contract, even if you weren't nurtured into it. For example, if the enemy has a generational contract of divination with a person's bloodline that is never directly addressed, it can manifest in a person's life without ever being introduced through parenting. My family is an example of this. I come from many generations of root workers and soothsayers. My grandmother was aware of this and purposely kept me far away from it, but because that agreement with divination was a part of my genetic coding, I always had an interest in the supernatural! Early in life, God showed me the root of this desire, and I broke the contract associated with my bloodline. Another example for me is gambling. I've always known that gambling has been a massive issue in my family, and because of that, I am prone to be very competitive when playing games. With that propensity in mind, I have made it my business never to involve money in competitions. My father never raised me to gamble, nor did he ever show me how to win, but I know what the enemy's assignment is to my family, so I don't give any room for the enemy to take advantage in my life. Nature generational curses can be a little more tricky to trace because they don't always directly involve your agreement. That's right: you can be affected by what your grandparents and their parents decided to agree with.

Numbers 14:18 (AMP)

18 'The Lord is slow to anger, and abundant in lovingkindness, forgiving wickedness and transgression; but He will by no means clear the guilty, visiting (avenging) the wickedness and guilt of the fathers on the children, to the third and fourth generations [that is, calling the children to account for the sins of their fathers].'

Do the math! You have two parents and each other; your parents have two parents and so on. If you go back four generations, that means that the decisions of at least 30 people could be positively or negatively affecting your life. If you are anything like me and there is a whole side of your family that you've never met, you can become obsessive about trying to track down the decisions of your ancestors but don't. You don't have to live under generational bondage. When you make Jesus the Lord of your life and receive his blood, you receive a spiritual blood transfusion. When you continually submit to Him in your mind, will, and emotions, you receive the heavenly benefits! Paul gives us some great news in Romans that should ease any worries you have about nature generational curses that may be active in your life or the lives of your loved ones.

Romans 8:17 (AMP)

17 And if [we are His] children, [then we are His] heirs also: heirs of God and fellow heirs with Christ [sharing His spiritual blessing and inheritance], if indeed we share in His suffering so that we may also share in His glory.

We are God's children, and when we agree with his plan for our lives and submit to His Son we become adopted into the fellowship of the beloved as sons and daughters of the Most High!

Once you become aware of the enemy's assignment to your family, you can almost always trace that to God's assignment for your family. The enemy attacks in the area where you're supposed to have the most authority. If you're going to be a successful deliverance minister, you must do an introspective study and comparison of your life. Re-examine the environments that you were nurtured in and ask yourself how this affected your life in a negative way. Inasmuch, look for genetic patterns and ask yourself: "How can I be the curse breaker?" It's an amazing thing to be able to promote freedom on behalf of God's kingdom to people whom you don't know, but it's better when you can bring your family out of bondage with you. Generational curses cannot stay active in the lives of people who decide to make a change. When you make the move to fully agree with what God said about your life, you will have power over every generational contract, no matter if it's nurture-driven or nature-driven. Destroying generational contracts can be difficult for many people because it requires you to face the comfortable bondages in your own life, but it also demands that you face your family dysfunctions!

Though the bible does not explicitly use the term *generational curse*, we see many examples of generational curses and their principles in the scripture. We saw it with Hezekiah in 2 Kings 20. Hezekiah made a bad decision, and the punishment for his actions were assigned to his children. We also have to acknowledge the fact that generational blessings are passed down in scripture. We see with Isaac and Jacob, and Esau and also the 12 sons of Israel that the father passes down a blessing to his sons! Generational curses cannot stay active without agreement or ignorance.

Proverbs 26:2 (NLT)

2 Like a fluttering sparrow or a darting swallow, an undeserved curse will not land on its intended victim.

This scripture shows us that curses cannot just fall on random people. There has to be a cause for it to stick. This means that the decisions we make in our life will directly affect our children and grandchildren. You can be the change that your family needs! All it requires is agreement with heaven! What anointing did God give your family? What is your family called to conquer? While on this journey to expand the kingdom of God, you must be intentional about spreading the truth to people who share your legacy!

In Acts, Jesus told His disciples that they had to be witnesses for Him.

Acts 1:8 (KJV)

8 But ye shall receive power, after that the Holy Ghost is come upon you: and ye shall be witnesses unto me both in Jerusalem, and in all Judaea, and in Samaria, and unto the uttermost part of the earth.

The first place Jesus told His disciples to carry the power that He gave them was to their family. Many of us have gotten it twisted. We think that the Lord is going to make us amazing deliverance ministers and then send us to the nations. That's admirable, but it's not the pattern Jesus laid out in His instructions. I believe that a training ground for your anointing and your character is learning to minister to the people in your family. Jerusalem was the first stop for the disciples because that's where they were from! That's where Jesus spent a great deal of His time ministering.

In other words, minister to your bloodline first. Cast the devil out of your family first. Break your generational curses first then go over to Judea, which represents friends, acquaintances, and people in your community. Judea was very close to Jerusalem and the people of both areas regularly communed with one another. Jesus thickened the plot though. He said to take that same power and purge yourself from your opinion and go and minister in Samaria, which represents your foes, enemies or people of different backgrounds and perspectives. The Jews and the Samaritans lived in hostility with one another because the Jews considered the Samaritans as unclean half breeds. If you are going to be effective in deliverance ministry, you can't skip this pattern. What generational curses are connected to YOUR Jerusalem? Will you be the curse breaker? Will you be the one that makes a stand in your Judea? Can you put your differences aside and extend some power to the people in your Samaria? Start within yourself and you can take it to the uttermost parts of the world!

Chapter Five
Workbook Section

Carve out some time in the notes section and document both your paternal and maternal family, sharing both family's life stories. After identifying the generational curses and the blessings within your family, how have those curses and blessings affected you? This should identify the history of strongholds from as far back as you can. Partner with the Holy Spirit to gain insight. Create a quiet space for you to focus. Stay in tune to thoughts, pictures, and feelings as you answer the questions below. The Holy Spirit speaks in a number of ways.

Ask the Holy Spirit this question and wait for answer: "Holy Spirit, what generational curses are active in my life right now?" Be patient and open to his voice.

Pray the following prayers to rid yourself of those curses:

1. I confess and repent of the sins of my ancestors (ask the Holy Spirit to reveal any in particular), my parents, and my own sin of _____. I repent of any anger and resentment that I have against You, God, for allowing this in my life.

2. I forgive and release my ancestors for passing on to me this sin and for the resulting curses of _____. (Be specific and ask the Lord for any revelation.) I ask You to forgive me for my participation in this sin. I receive Your forgiveness. I forgive myself for participating in this sin.

Chapter 6
The Anatomy of Soul Ties

As we continue to explore the ways the enemy gains access to our lives, it's imperative that we take an in-depth look at soul ties. As discussed before, the enemy is a legalist. He doesn't have the authority to access our lives on his own. He is weak and therefore requires human consent to work in the earth realm. Soul ties are a major loophole that he uses to bind up believers. Deliverance is not just a spiritual issue. Deliverance is an issue of the soul! Traditionally, when we think about soul ties, we automatically think about sex, but soul ties are much more complex than sex. In order to understand soul ties, we must first understand what the soul is. For the last two years, I have had an aggressive burden to understand the soul more deeply. My study time with the Holy Spirit on this topic has given me a great deal of revelation on the functionality of the soul. It has shown me the dangers of being unaware of the condition of our soul. The soul of a human being is more important than we think. Every day all over this world, people travel to see a therapist, psychologist, priest, and pastor to talk about their issues with deep emotional pain, mental trauma, and uncontrollable desires. People are continually searching for a way to manage the soul, but we have forgotten that when we want to fix something, we should go back to the source of its creation. Be mindful that the soul of man came from the spirit of God. Now, that sounds really simple when you first glance at it, but let's take a more in-depth look.

Genesis 2:7 (KJV)

7 And the Lord God formed man of the dust of the ground and breathed into his nostrils the breath of life, and man became a living soul.

God did something to man that He didn't do to any of His other creations. The first thing that He did differently was that He formed man from the dust of the earth. Then the second thing that He did was He blew the spirit of life into his nostrils and man became a living soul. The soul of man came out of the spirit of God. This makes man different from any other creation. The soul of man came from the spirit of God, so it must return to the spirit of God for restoration! Man is a spirit, but he has a soul. Angels are spirits, but I do not believe they possess a soul. The soul has been given to us because we have been given freedom of choice and freedom to create! When God decided to make man, He wanted to give man the capacity to commune with Him, and the only way the eternal spirit of God could connect with the finite spirit of man is by making man in His image! God gave man the ability to think, feel, and choose his way into a relationship with God the Father!

The soul is comprised of three distinct attributes: the mind, will, and emotions. Understanding each part of the soul will allow us to see where and why ties happen. A soul tie is a linkage in the soulish realm between an individual, an idea, an organization, or another person. Soul ties can link two souls and bring forth beneficial results or negative results. Soul ties between two people develop with vulnerability, intimacy, and a loss of boundaries.

Boundaries are in place to protect the future of your soul! Your soul is the most important thing in your life, and every relationship you enter into must benefit your destiny, or you will create unhealthy expectations! Without boundaries relationships, don't have definition. Without definition, a relationship won't have a purpose! Negative soul ties are created when boundaries aren't established or respected. There are a number of things that break down boundaries. Broken boundaries lead to tied souls! Here are a few signs that your boundaries are being broken:

1) When you start making excuses for someone's behavior.
2) When you start trivializing your time and energy.
3) When you allow sin to separate you from God.
4) When there is progressive irreverence for the mental, emotional, and physical health of another person.
5) When you are continually let by your carnal senses.

The kingdom of darkness is strategic and is always trying to sabotage your progress and future by getting you to attach to the wrong things. When boundaries are broken, space for the demonic realm to advance is created.

Soul ties are created through intimacy, and intimacy is more than sex. Intimacy is letting a person into your goals, apprehensions, and struggles. In other words, welcoming people to see your naked truth is intimacy. In building healthy relationships, vulnerability is so important, but you have to be careful whom you are vulnerable with. When sharing your traumas with people who don't share your convictions, you open the door for your mind, will, and emotions to be tethered to a perspective that does not support growth.

When your mind is tied to another person, your perspective of the world is connected and influenced by his/her perspective. People who have soul ties don't think properly. I like to call this area of the soul tie a mind-tie. They get stuck in mentally abusive and manipulative relationships, but because they "feel" connected to that person they allow the truth of their abuse to be irrationally rationalized. They make excuses for every offense. Mind ties are strongest in places of fantasy and in places of memory. This is why it is so important to never invest in a relationship that was not born in the will of God! I have had many occasions where people want to break free from deception, but they don't because they have put their hope in a fantasy of what the relationship could be.

Another link in soul ties are emotions. I have heard testimony of people's souls being so bound to each other that they knew what a person was feeling without having natural communication with him/her. This type of connection is soulish and dangerous, especially when it's with someone who is not your destiny partner. I have counseled many people who considered an emotional connection as a sign from God that they were supposed to be with a person. Emotions are not meant to be a guide for us; they are designed to be a gauge for our needs, hurts, and issues. When you allow your emotions to lead your decision making, you'll always find yourself doing what you feel, but just because you feel something doesn't mean that it's the right thing to do. All emotions should be filtered through Holy Spirit. Emotion is a fundamental component of all intimate relations. Negative emotions can present a signal that something is not going well in the relationship, motivating you to change. However, in soul ties, the drive for change is ignored! It is necessary to permit yourself to feel these adverse emotions when they arise and to deal with them in a healthy way.

The final major factor in soul ties is the will. When in a soul tie, your desires are all out of whack. Soul ties make you desire a relationship with a person, even when everything about that person is dangerous. I have helped countless people get free from soul ties where they mentally knew the relationship was dangerous and they emotionally were terrified of the individual but they still desired the other person in their core. This desire is strongest when the focus is on the pleasure that a person gives you more than the pain he/she causes. We are designed for intimacy but at different levels with different relationships. If you are going to be effective in deliverance ministry, you must be prepared for the bloody battle that comes with soul ties.

In the following chapter, you will learn how to break soul ties through breaking legal ground, but before you get there you should ask Holy Spirit to heal your memory and free you from any fantasy that has your soul tied to anything.

Chapter Six
Workbook Section

Exercise: In the notes section, explain the three parts of the soul and how they should align with God!

1. Where did the soul of a man originate?

_____

_____

_____

_____

2. How do boundaries help us maintain a healthy soul?

_____

_____

_____

_____

_____

_____

_____

3. What are some signs of broken boundaries? Identify areas you have possibly displayed broken boundaries that lead to an unhealthy soul tie.

_____

_____

_____

_____

_____

_____

_____

_____

_____

_____

_____

_____

Chapter Seven
Breaking Legal Ground

In deliverance, one of the most important subjects you must have an understanding of is legal ground. I mentioned earlier that demons are legalistic. This means they can only operate within certain parameters. Demons can't freely move and terrorize, so they enter this world by creating contracts and/or agreements with people who choose to believe their lies! Demons can only operate in areas of our lives that we allow them to. They are spirits that belong in the spirit world. They don't have bodies which means they don't legally have the right to operate in our realm. God gave the earth to humankind.

Psalm 115:15-16 (AMP)
15 May you be blessed of the Lord, Who made heaven and earth.16 The heavens are the heavens of the Lord, But the earth He has given to the children of men.

Demons create their rights by building detailed contracts with us that allow them to gain entry into this world. These contracts include, but are not limited to, occult involvement, participation in other religions, soul ties (sexual and non-sexual), unforgiveness, bitter-root judgements, self-imposed vows, and word curses. Demons will not leave easily unless the contracts have been broken. You can still command demons to leave without breaking legal ground, but that can turn into a long, messy, violent battle.

It's also dangerous for the person receiving ministry. When legal ground is not broken and a demon is forced out, it can cause a person physical agony as it leaves. In addition, the demon will come back!

Luke 11:24-26 (AMP)

24 "When the unclean spirit comes out of a person, it roams through waterless places in search [of a place] of rest; and not finding any, it says, 'I will go back to my house (person) from which I came.' 25 And when it comes, it finds the place swept and put in order. 26 Then it goes and brings seven other spirits more evil than itself, and they go in [the person] and live there; and the last state of that person becomes worse than the first."

It is irresponsible of you to cast the demon out of someone who doesn't agree or understand because that demon is going to come back with reinforcement and according to scripture the ending state will be worse than the beginning. During a deliverance session, one of the first things you need to do is break all legal ground and contracts. This is done by having the deliverance recipient repent, renounce, confess, and forgive. It is imperative that the prayers of repentance, renunciation, and forgiveness be prayed by the person receiving deliverance. He/she must come into agreement with Christ, making an announcement to the demons oppressing his/her life that he/she desires freedom.

These prayers, coupled with the decision to be free, will destroy every bit of legal ground the enemy has stood on, making room for Holy Spirit to fill the places that were once occupied by the demonic. Breaking legal ground demands complete honesty. The enemy uses shame to cause people to conceal their bondage which inhibits them from being free. You must create an environment that is completely confidential and free of judgment. People will be honest when they trust that you are just as invested in their freedom as they are.

Repentance is important because it opens the door for God to come into an area that was previously restricted. Be careful not to get pulled into doing deliverance on people who haven't fully decided to turn away from their bondage.

2 Corinthians 7:10 (NLT)

10 For the kind of sorrow God wants us to experience leads us away from sin and results in salvation. There's no regret for that kind of sorrow. But worldly sorrow, which lacks repentance, results in spiritual death.

At least two times every week, I am asked to conduct personal deliverance sessions. I don't take 90% of these requests because most people have not reached a place of Godly sorrow about their bondage. Deliverance is for the decided and desperate. Some people want partial deliverance. They will repent for some things but are unwilling to turn away from the sinful things they still enjoy. These people are the most dangerous deliverance candidates, and I don't recommend entertaining their desire for partial deliverance. You can't cry for Jesus to be Savior and not allow Him to be Lord.

According to Acts 2:38, Jesus calls us to repentance. It is by repentance that God gives us a change of mind. Repentance opens the door to closed areas in our thinking and allows the freshness of God to breathe into us. We are then able to ward off the attacks of the enemy.

You will know when people are truly desperate for deliverance or if they just want attention. People who are truly desperate for change will be willing to do whatever they need to do to be free. True repentance leads to deliverance. Repenting is our way of serving the enemy an eviction notice. It alerts him that some things are about to change.

Demons thrive in darkness and secrecy. They manifest during strong and anointed teaching because biblical teaching reveals truth. This kind of teaching shines a light into the darkness within us and causes us to realize areas where change needs to happen. It's necessary to repent of all known and unknown sins.

Forgiveness is often the most important part of breaking legal ground. When people start to forgive, you may notice demonic manifestations. Holding unforgiveness in one's heart is a form of pride, and according to James 4:6, God resists the proud. Forgiveness is a decision.

When you choose to forgive, you willingly release the offender from the offense. Forgiveness is sometimes more difficult when the offender refuses to acknowledge his/her wrong, repeatedly offends you, or passes the blame to you. However, forgiveness is essential to true freedom

Mark 11:25-26 (AMP)

25 Whenever you stand praying, if you have anything against anyone, forgive him [drop the issue, let it go], so that your Father who is in heaven will also forgive you your transgressions and wrongdoings [against Him and others]. 26 [But if you do not forgive, neither will your Father in heaven forgive your transgressions."]

When a person refuses to release offense, he/she blocks the delivering power of Christ. According to this passage in Mark, God will not forgive us if we don't forgive those who have offended us. No matter how hard it is, we have to accept that forgiveness is a crucial component of operating in authority. Sometimes we make the decision to forgive, but seeing the offender rekindles the painful emotions of the offense. The enemy will tell you that you haven't forgiven but that is not true! Forgiveness is not about a feeling. When you choose to forgive a person, you must then command your emotions to align with your decision.

There was a time when I was doing a session on a young man who had a very abusive past. The demons were coming out pretty quickly and smoothly until I started calling out trauma. At that point, he began to shake and growl violently. I was completely thrown off, but God showed me a vision of a rug with the word *unforgiveness* sewn into it. I saw a very stubborn spirit standing on the rug with his arms folded, refusing to move. I stopped the session and asked if there was someone he hadn't forgiven in relation to the abuse. He couldn't think of anyone. Holy Spirit said, "He must forgive himself in order to be free!" I took him through prayers of self-forgiveness, and he was instantly set free. We must forgive everyone who has offended us in any way.

Confession shines the light into the enemies dark plans. It dismantles the strength of stealth. The enemy is a master of secrecy and deception. Secrecy is a very strong contract to break with people who are ashamed about their bondage. Most of the time people who have been raised under strict religious households struggle to actually confess their sins. Demons will replay a person's mistake in their mind and influence them to feel shame. The enemy doesn't just want you to feel bad about your mistakes; he wants you to own them as a part of your identity. Instead of planting thoughts like: "I fornicated," demons go the extra mile to make you think: " I am a fornicator, and I shouldn't tell anyone!"

James 5:16 (AMP)
16 Therefore, confess your sins to one another [your false steps, your offenses], and pray for one another, that you may be healed and restored. The heartfelt and persistent prayer of a righteous man (believer) can accomplish much [when put into action and made effective by God—it is dynamic and can have tremendous power].

Confessing your sin to someone else while having a sincere desire to be free will break the enemy's contracts and usher in deliverance! In most cases, a refusal to confess is a sign of shame.

In a session, you should remind the person that Christ already knows what he/she has done and that Christ has already forgiven him/her. When he/she confesses his/her wrong(s), he/she should then confess Christ as his/her Lord and Savior. One reason that many people struggle with confession is that it opens the door to accountability. When you tell the truth about what's going on with you, it gives your Christian brothers and sisters access to help you.

During a previous session, one young man was so ashamed of his sexual impurities that he covered his face to try to avoid confessing them. Confessing faults makes things real for many people. People can hold the memory for many years and never speak on it, but when they confess their sins the severity of their need for Christ becomes apparent! Confession uncovers hidden demons. Remember, the enemy operates in secrecy; God doesn't. God deals in mystery, and if you seek Him, He will reveal hidden things. Secrets are meant to be kept hidden, but mysteries are an invitation to go deeper in your relationship with God. Confess all your sins, and watch God flood that area with freedom and healing.

Renunciations are especially important for people who have been in blatant rebellion against God by way of other religions, occult activity, and alternative lifestyles. To renounce means to formally declare that you will no longer engage in or support something. We renounce things like generational curses, familiar spirits, and self-imposed vows. Demons are detail-oriented, and if you leave any space for them, they will take it.

I had to intentionally renounce all works of witchcraft that were associated with my bloodline. I have never been actively involved in witchcraft, but one of my ancestors made an agreement with a spirit of divination. That pattern can be traced throughout my family tree. You repent to God; you renounce to the demonic world. Breaking legal ground can take time, but it is definitely worth it. It helps people identify faulty thought patterns and makes for a more thorough cleansing in deliverance. When people are able to pinpoint what caused their pain, they are more prone to seal the door shut!

Chapter Seven
Workbook Section

1. Check every tool used to break legal ground.

    a. __Prophecy
    b. __Forgiveness
    c. __Thankfulness
    d. __Confession
    e. __Repentance
    f. __Counseling
    g. __Renunciation

2. In the process of administering deliverance, what is the first step?

_____

_____

_____

3. Why is deliverance ministry without repentance impossible? In the notes section, write out 2-3 scriptures that support your answer.

_____

_____

_____

_____

_____

_____

_____

_____

_____

4. How are unforgiveness and pride correlated, and how do they stifle your ability to see deliverance?

_____

_____

_____

_____

_____

_____

_____

_____

5. How does confession break the power of shame? Why is this intricate in the deliverance process?

_____

_____

_____

_____

_____

_____

_____

_____

_____

6. What does the enemy need in order to operate in the earth realm?

   (Check all that apply)

   a. __A body
   b. __The agreement of mankind
   c. __Deception
   d. __Money
   e. __Witches

7. What is the definition of *renunciation*? In the notes section, name 1-3 ways you have rebelled against God and how the power of renunciation can help alleviate their power.

   _____

   _____

   _____

   _____

   _____

   _____

   _____

   _____

   _____

   _____

Exercise: Take a moment and ask the Holy Spirit to help you recall the individuals and events in your life that have caused you pain. If you have an offense, you must forgive.

In the notes section, write out this exercise for every person. Make sure you take time and forgive yourself as well.

Place each person in the following template:

"I forgive____ for ___" (*ex: I forgive my mother for never understanding me.*) Go down the list of people who are associated which each event.

_____

_____

_____

_____

_____

_____

_____

_____

_____

_____

Chapter Eight
Prayer

Prayer is one of the most potent weapons that you will use against the enemy. Prayer is not only the way that we communicate with God, but it is also the way we become sensitive to what God is saying and doing. When we pray, our hearts become knit with His! This is important because you must feel God's heart towards every person receiving deliverance. Deliverance is not about a show of strength; it is an act of God's love. If you don't pray, you won't have the capacity for compassion every deliverance minister must have. The greatest weapon of attack is prayer.

James 5:16 (AMP)

16 Therefore, confess your sins to one another [your false steps, your offenses], and pray for one another, that you may be healed and restored. <u>The heartfelt and persistent prayer of a righteous man (believer) can accomplish much [when put into action and made effective by God—it is dynamic and can have tremendous power]</u>.

Prayer is an integral way that we unweave the contracts created through legal ground. We must always remember that the ability to destroy the works of the enemy comes from God. Our prayers activate His power in us. As a deliverance minister, you must be skilled in a few different types of prayers.

Communion/Worship- This is prayer between you and God. As I mentioned earlier, there is no way for you to be effective in deliverance without communing with the source of delivering power. This prayer is where you dedicate specific time to God for yourself! You don't go into this type of prayer asking for anything; you enter prayers of communion for your mind and heart to be knit with God's. When you enter into worship with God, you will become more aware of what is on His heart.

John 4:24 (AMP)

24 God is spirit [the Source of life, yet invisible to mankind], and those who worship Him must worship in spirit and truth."

Intercession- Becoming a deliverance minister is one of the most powerful forms of intercession. To intercede means to stand in the gap. Your job is to get in between the person you are praying for and whatever is tormenting them. Your job is to lead them in prayers, but in some cases you will have to step in and pray on their behalf! Jesus prayed prayers of intercession, and so should we!

Luke 22:31-32 (AMP)

31 "Simon, Simon (Peter), listen! Satan has demanded permission to sift [all of] you like grain; 32 but I have prayed [especially] for you [Peter], that your faith [and confidence in Me] may not fail; and you, once you have turned back again [to Me], strengthen and support your brothers [in the faith]."

Petition- Prayers of petition are used to ask God to meet a need. In a deliverance session, you will need a lot of things: strength, insight, clarity, and courage. Never allow yourself to hit a wall where you get lost and don't pray for direction! The enemy can be tricky, and he has stamina. Prayers of petition will help you walk through every attack. Pray and believe God will meet your needs.

Luke 11:9 Amplified Bible (AMP)

9 "So I say to you, ask and keep on asking, and it will be given to you; seek and keep on seeking, and you will find; knock and keep on knocking, and the door will be opened to you.

Agreement- Something amazing happens when believers come together in agreement to pray. Jesus taught us that when we join together to ask anything of God, He would be with us and answer our prayers. This is good for deliverance because you should never do a deliverance session on your own. You need someone there to agree with you!

Matthew 18:19-20 (AMP)

19 "Again I say to you, that if two believers on earth agree [that is, are of one mind, in harmony] about anything that they ask [within the will of God], it will be done for them by My Father in heaven. 20 For where two or three are gathered in My name [meeting together as My followers], I am there among them."

Praying in Tongues- Praying in tongues is a powerful tool in deliverance. I do not believe that you should pray every prayer in tongues because it is important for the person receiving deliverance to understand what's going on and being said. You pray to build yourself up for war. Praying in tongues connects you with Holy Spirit and allows His power to work through you. Here is a disclaimer: demons are not afraid of your tongues. They respond to the word of God and the name of Jesus Christ.

1 Corinthians 14:14-15(AMP)
14 For if I pray in a tongue, my spirit prays, but my mind is unproductive [because it does not understand what my spirit is praying]. 15 Then what am I to do? I will pray with the spirit [by the Holy Spirit that is within me] and I will pray with the mind [using words I understand]; I will sing with the spirit [by the Holy Spirit that is within me] and I will sing with the mind [using words I understand].

Also, in Ephesians 6:18, Paul, after listing the six defensive portions of the armor of God, listed an offensive strategy for spiritual warfare.

Ephesians 6:18 (AMP)
18 With all prayer and petition pray [with specific requests] at all times [on every occasion and in every season] in the Spirit, and with this in view, stay alert with all perseverance and petition [interceding in prayer] for all God's people.

Binding and Loosing- I believe that binding and loosing are the most important prayers for every deliverance minister. They should be practiced in every session. This is the way we exercise our authority over the kingdom of darkness. Jesus said that He has given us authority over all the authority of the enemy, which means that we can command the enemy to leave us alone!

Matthew 16:19 Amplified Bible (AMP)

19 I will give you the keys (authority) of the kingdom of heaven; and whatever you bind [forbid, declare to be improper and unlawful] on earth will have [already] been bound in heaven, and whatever you loose [permit, declare lawful] on earth will have [already] been loosed in heaven."

This scripture tells us that we are backed by all of heaven when we are submitted to God. When we stand as deliverance ministers, we stand representing the might of God's kingdom. What we arrest on earth is arrested in heaven, and what we permit on earth is permitted in heaven.

Remember this: you must know the word of God when you pray. You can't represent heaven and not know heaven's orders. Demons do not respond to book knowledge or experiences. When you pray, you must pray the words of the person whom you represent or you won't get much response. When praying for peace, you should quote scriptures about peace. When praying for deliverance, your prayer verbiage should be laced with what the Bible says about deliverance and salvation.

Guided Prayer: Father, I thank You for Your Son Jesus who made it possible for us to stand before Your throne and make declarations. You said in Your word that we have been given the keys to the kingdom, and when we bind things on earth, they are bound in heaven. Right now, I stand with that authority, and I bind the works of every spirit that comes to promote torment, depression, and anxiety. I loose peace into that place, in the name of Jesus.

Chapter Eight
Workbook Section

1. How do intercession and deliverance go hand in hand?

_____

_____

_____

_____

_____

_____

_____

_____

2. Explain the prayer of binding and loosing.

_____

_____

_____

_____

_____

_____

_____

_____

_____

_____

_____

_____

3. How do worship and communion with the Holy Spirit enhance your ability to administer deliverance?

_____

_____

_____

_____

_____

_____

_____

_____

_____

_____

_____

_____

_____

_____

Exercise: In the notes section, reflect over the exercise where you were asked to partner with the Holy Spirit to help you recall the individuals and events in your life that caused you pain. Write out a prayer of intercession for the person who has offended you the most. (Ask God to show you His heart and good intentions towards them).

In the notes section, write your own breaking legal ground prayer.

_____

_____

_____

_____

_____

_____

_____

_____

_____

_____

_____

_____

Chapter Nine
Demonic Manifestation

When most people think about demonic manifestations, they think about someone's head spinning around or someone throwing up green stuff. They think about someone speaking in another language and being uncontrollable. The enemy has infiltrated the media with fear! Movies, television shows, and web series have all made the kingdom of darkness seem more powerful than it really is! Uncontrolled demonic manifestations are an enemy to deliverance ministers. One of the main reasons churches do not flow in deliverance and actively call out the devil is because they fear manifestations. Demons are not wild animals. They are strategic beings, and everything they do has a purpose.

Demons manifest for a number of reasons. They manifest to distract, challenge authority, and incite fear. They also manifest when their time has come to be cast out. Never forget that you have the authority to make manifestations stop! I believe the church has lost interest in going toe to toe with demons because we don't teach repentance, confession, and forgiveness anymore. When you refuse to take time and break legal ground, you can have very strong and spooky manifestations, and most churches aren't prepared to deal with that. Jesus always commanded demons to stop acting out, and you should too!

Luke 4:35 (AMP)

35 But Jesus rebuked him, saying, "Be silent (muzzled, gagged) and come out of him!" And when the demon had thrown the man down among them, he came out of him without injuring him in any way.

Jesus taught with authority, and the demon recognized it! I believe that this demon manifested to distract those who were listening to Jesus. The church is the representation of God's authority on the earth. We must cast out demons with the power that comes from God. Demonic manifestations are not something that you take time to analyze or gaze at with awe. You must quickly address them and bring them under subjection. Demons will ask challenging questions to test your faith!

I was recently praying at the altar with a woman. When I began to call out spirits, a demon (in an attempt to shake my faith) spoke through her and said, "Who is this Lord you speak of?" I replied, "You know who Jesus is. At His name, every knee must bow and every tongue must confess that He is Lord. Now confess that Jesus is Lord." When I commanded the demon to make that confession, it screamed and squirmed because it knew its time was up.

There are many common manifestations around the altar or in a personal deliverance session. Remember, never attempt to box demons into your personal experiences. You must allow every encounter with the demonic to be led by Holy Spirit. He is a revealer of all truth. Demons also manifest as they leave. Manifestations can include, but are not limited to:

Shaking- This can be a sign that the demon is afraid of being cast out. I have experienced demons tremble in fear when hearing Jesus' name.

Physical Pain- Most times when a person receiving deliverance is experiencing pain, it is a sign of a spirit of infirmity. However, it can also be a sign of unbroken legal ground.

Choking- Sometimes as demons are leaving through the throat or the nose, it will choke a person in an attempt to hold on to its place.

Burping, Yawning, or Deep Breathing- Demons are spirits and the Greek word for spirit is *pneuma,* which translates to air. Some of the most common signs that demons are leaving are breathing, yawning, burping, and passing gas.

Coughing- Sometimes demons of death and the occult will hide in the lung area. When they are called out, they will cause the person to cough.

Movements in the Body- It is very common for people to feel movement in their stomach, back, legs, or arms when demons are leaving.

Weakness- Demons can cause people to feel weak during sessions. This is sometimes a way for them to gain sympathy to end the session, but you must command weakness to stop!

Flinching- Sometimes as spirits are leaving, they will cause certain areas of a person's body to twitch involuntarily.

Screaming- Deliverance sessions can be very loud, and one common manifestation is screaming. This is usually a sign of deep emotional pain.

Spitting or Purging- As demons begin to vacate, people will sometimes purge or cough up bodily fluids. Because of this, it is important to keep tissue, hand sanitizer, and trash bags on hand when administering deliverance.

Growling, Barking, or Hissing- These manifestations are a direct attempt to scare or challenge the authority of the deliverance minister. Remind the demonic spirits that all power has been given to you through Jesus Christ and command it to stop!

Pungent Odors- I have experienced many sessions where demons cause a smell to come into the room. Don't be alarmed. Call the spirit out!

Talking- Demons will talk through a person when you are casting them out. I do not ever recommend holding conversations with demons. Demons are liars, so I don't believe in asking demons for any kind of information. When you need to know a demon's name or how it entered, you should ask Holy Spirit. Sometimes demons will scream their names as they leave.

Always encourage the person receiving deliverance to breathe and receive. Some people will try to pray and speak in tongues, but you should encourage them to simply breathe and receive. I also recommend that you encourage them to keep their eyes open so that they are aware of what is going on. Demons are never in control; as the deliverance minister, you are in control. Furthermore, just because a demon is manifesting doesn't mean that it is coming out.

When you come up against uncontrollable manifestations, you should stop the session and revisit areas of legal ground. Bitterness, unforgiveness, pride, and dishonesty can be hindrances to freedom, making the sessions extremely laborious. I have witnessed cases wherein people have felt demons move from one place in their body to another in order to avoid expulsion.

A lady once came to me after a mass deliverance session and mentioned that she had experienced a great deal of freedom but felt like a spirit had hidden in her upper back. I placed my hands on the area and commanded the spirit to leave. As the spirit came out, I felt the spirit pass my hand as if it were a hard lump.

Lastly, never allow a demon to be a distraction to service. If a demonic manifestation occurs during a worship experience, continue to worship so that God can be exalted. Don't ever stop worship to deal with a demon. Call the manifestations under subjections or take them to another room to deal with them.

Chapter Nine
Workbook Section

1. List some common reasons demons manifest.

_____

_____

_____

_____

_____

_____

_____

_____

_____

_____

_____

_____

2. What is the difference between a stronghold and a strongman?

_____

_____

_____

_____

_____

_____

_____

3. How should deliverance ministers handle demonic manifestations?

_____

_____

_____

_____

_____

_____

_____

4. Explain the components of a demonic stronghold.

_____

_____

_____

_____

_____

_____

_____

5. How did Jesus respond to demonic manifestations?

_____

_____

_____

_____

_____

_____

_____

Chapter Ten
Word Curses

Words are vessels filled with spiritual power! There is a famous myth that when the Solomon Islands of the pacific islanders want to cut down an enormous tree that seems challenging to chop down, they perform a special kind of curse: a word curse. When you search for it on Google, researchers refer to it as curse magic. These islanders use word curses like Jesus did when he was disappointed by the fig tree.

According to the myth, the people of the Solomon Islands yell and say negative things, at the top of their voices, to the trees. As a result of this word curse, the tree dies and falls to the ground in some days—many studies and experiments on plants in which the same plants were placed in three separate rooms. In one room, kind words were spoken; in the second, harsh words were spoken, and there was pin-drop silence in the third room. The results showed that the plants which were exposed to kind words grew a little more than the other two. What does it show?

It shows us that words are powerful. If they can affect plants, imagine their impact on humans who can comprehend what's being said. When we speak, the sound waves carry the message spoken and carry the spirit in which we spoke the words in to impact the person on the receiving end. At times, this impact lasts forever. The problem occurs when the words are poisonous. They become a parasitic plant that resides inside that person, and they try to eat away at his/her soul. Word curses are real!

During my years in deliverance ministry, I have come to realize the true power of words. Word curses are one of the most common yet powerful tools that the enemy uses to create contractual agreements with God's people. I have seen people speak words out of bitterness and anger to each other! I've heard people say things out of hate, and the results are devastating to the soul. The weight of the harm isn't in the initial contact but the way the words linger and fester. Word curses aren't hard to identify. They can be subtle or strong, but their goal is the same to wound the soul!

The bible records history of people who sent and received blessings and curses through their words. The bible speaks of the tremendous power of words, both for good and evil, for blessing and cursing. For instance, God spoke creation into existence. His words have ultimate power and authority. Since we are created in the image of God, it stands to reason that our words also carry power. Here are a few biblical examples:

1. "Death and life are in the power of the tongue." Proverbs 18:21
2. "For whoever would love life and see good days must keep their tongue from evil and their lips from deceitful speech." 1 Peter 3:10
3. "Not what goes into the mouth defiles a man; but what comes out of the mouth, this defiles a man." Matthew 15:11
4. "Keep your tongue from evil and your lips from speaking deceit." Psalm 34:13

5. "But no human being can tame the tongue. It is a restless evil, full of deadly poison." James 3:8

Word curses manifest in various ways but be sure that this is not some superstitious or primitive belief. The bible speaks about blessings and curses, and these are both real forces in the world. Words are powerful by themselves, but what enhances the power of word curses is when the person on the receiving end values the person speaking the curse. What empowers a word curse to be active in one's life is believing what's being said about him/her. If you want to destroy word curses, here are a few steps you can take.

1. Identify the word curses/negative words spoken by others or self.
2. Forgive and repent for speaking curses and forgive those who spoke those curses over you, including yourself.
3. Break all agreements with those word curses in the name of Jesus Christ.
4. Believe that the curse HAS BEEN REVERSED and is no longer operational.
5. Begin to make verbal declarations to counteract any word curse. For example, if you were affected by a curse that said you were not smart you should verbally declare that you are brilliant in Jesus' name!
6. Remember Romans 12:2, "And do not be conformed to this world, but be transformed by the renewing of your mind, that

you may prove what is that good and acceptable and perfect will of God."

Chapter Ten
Workbook Section

1. Identify word curses in your life that others have spoken against you and you have spoken against yourself. How have these curses impacted your life and destiny?

_____

_____

_____

_____

_____

_____

_____

_____

_____

2. How are word curses activated?

_____

_____

_____

_____

_____

_____

3. In the notes section, list the most significant word curses. For each one of those curses, write a declaration of blessing over yourself along with scriptures to counteract it! Make these daily affirmations to build your identity and confidence.

_____

_____

_____

_____

_____

_____

_____

_____

Chapter Eleven
Deliverance Step-by-Step

You will not always have the perfect environment for deliverance, and you will not always be able to follow all of these steps in this order. The purpose of this book is not to give you a cookie-cutter way to perform deliverance ministry. Instead, it is meant to give you information and parameters that promote healthy experiences with the Holy Spirit. I'm going to give you what I believe are the steps to a successful spirit-led deliverance session. This is not the only way to do deliverance. Feel free to adjust or add as led by Holy Spirit.

In this chapter, I will provide instructions for altar ministry and personal sessions. Personal sessions should never replace professional Christian counseling nor should counseling sessions replace personal deliverance. Deliverance and counseling go hand in hand. Once you cast the devil out of someone's mind, he/she will need to be retrained in his/her thinking. This can be done through counseling, discipleship, and accountability.

Altar deliverance is an abbreviated version of a personal session. You don't get to take as much time to break legal ground. Normally, you will have less than twenty minutes to pray with someone. Don't try to call out every demon in that time frame. Altar deliverance can get chaotic if you don't retain focus.

Personal Deliverance Sessions

Step 1) Prepare for Deliverance- You should never work deliverance on your own. In personal sessions, a team of 2 or 3 people per person is ideal. All team members should take time with Holy Spirit, pray in tongues, and ask God for insight to help the person obtain freedom. Be aware: personal session times can vary. I've been in sessions as short as one hour and as long as five hours. Session times depend on the person receiving deliverance. My personal practice is to get through as much as possible in 2 hours.

Step 2) Interview the Candidate- This part of the process requires you to ask very personal questions regarding the candidate's need for deliverance. Ask questions about his/her family, church/religious background, sexual activity, occult involvement, beliefs about the bible, sin patterns, and prior experience with deliverance.

The purpose of these questions is not to get into the candidate's business but to identify areas of legal ground. I suggest creating a questionnaire to be sent to everyone who requests deliverance. Doing so will drastically reduce the interview time during your sessions.

Guided Example: Dottie comes for deliverance because she deals with intense anxiety and a fear of death. Through the interview, you find that she has lost her mother in a tragic accident. You could identify the entry point for the spirit of fear as coming from the trauma of the tragic loss.

Step 3) Covering Prayer- This prayer allows you to set spiritual boundaries. I recommend that you and your team take time to pray in tongues and then pray a simple prayer of covering. Remember, you have the authority.

Guided Covering Prayer (Say out loud)- Father, You are full of grace and truth. You are the creator of all and the source of all authority! I praise You for allowing Your Son Jesus to come to earth and shed His blood for our sins. I repent now for all known and unknown sins I have committed and I ask that Your Son's blood be applied over my life and the lives of every person in this room. I pray that the blood covers us from all backlash and attachment, and I decree and declare that every spirit that leaves this place goes to the dry places never to return again, in the name of Jesus Christ.

Step 4) Breaking Legal Ground- As we discussed in Chapter Five, breaking legal ground is extremely important for every deliverance session. In this portion of the session, the candidate for deliverance has to be extremely invested and involved. He/she will pray prayers of confession, repentance, renunciation, and forgiveness to God the Father and ask Him to set him/her free. In the prayer, make sure he/she confesses that Jesus Christ is the

Lord of his/her entire life. Some points in the example prayer below will require acts of confession for them as well as on behalf of their entire family line.

Guided Legal Ground Prayer- Lord Jesus, You said in Your word that those who call upon You would be delivered, so I come now asking that You would deliver me. I establish Jesus Christ as my Lord and Savior. I confess that Jesus is the Son of God and has complete authority over my mind, body, soul, relationships, and life. I ask that You forgive me for all of my sins and the sins of my entire ancestral line. I confess that we have committed the sins of _____*(have them confess all known sins that they and their ancestors have committed. For example, if adultery runs in the family, have them confess it.)* On behalf of my entire family, I repent. I ask that You destroy all patterns of sin in my ancestral line all the way back to the beginning of time. I renounce any involvement in other religions that I or my ancestors have been involved in that do not acknowledge Jesus Christ as Lord. Lord, I confess that I have indulged in sexual immorality, and I ask that You forgive me of the following sexual sins _____*(Confess all sexual sin. Ex: fornication, pornography, etc.)* I pray that every soul tie that was a result of these sexual sins be broken by the power of Holy Spirit. I break every ungodly linking created between myself and_____ *(Call the names of people you have soul ties with. This includes ex-lovers, one night stands, and abusers.)* I pray that every part of my soul illegally tied to these people be snatched back to me in

114

Jesus' name. I repent and ask that You wash me with the waters of Your word. I repent for every word that I have spoken against people who have offended and hurt me. I pray that You would bless them and forgive me for every judgment I have spoken against them and the judgments that I have spoken against myself. I break every negative inner vow that I have declared over my life and destiny. Father, I pray that You would forgive me for all involvement in occult activities. I acknowledge that Your word identifies these things as sin, and I confess that I have participated in_____*(Ex: **tarot card readings, horoscopes, root working, etc.)*** Purge my soul from any residue of these things in Jesus' name. I thank You Lord that everything I have prayed has been answered because I have prayed it according to Your word and in Jesus' name. Amen.

Step 5) Forgiveness Prayer- Though prayers of forgiveness can be grouped with prayers to break legal ground, I separated it because demonic manifestations usually happen as soon as a person starts the forgiveness process. If this happens, you should command all manifestations to stop and push the person to complete the prayer. Forgiveness can be hard for many people. It is a good idea to remind them that forgiveness does not excuse the offender from the wrong; however, it is a declaration that they won't view life from the lens of offense any longer.

Guided Forgiveness Prayer- Father, I thank You for Your gift of forgiveness. You said in Your word that in order for us to receive forgiveness from You, we must forgive others. Your mercy flows to me in spite of my faults and failures, so I now extend that same mercy to every person who has offended me. I understand that even though I feel the pain of the offense, my emotions don't have to control my decision to forgive. Lord, I choose to see the people who have caused my pain as Your children, loved and accepted by You, and I ask You to help me find the compassion that comes with true forgiveness. I choose today to forgive _____*(insert person's name)* for _____*(insert offense) (Ex: I forgive Charles for stealing from me. Repeat this for every offender.)* I choose today to release each of these people from these offenses into the freedom of my forgiveness. I also release myself from being the victim any longer. I release myself from all woundedness and deep hurt tied to these situations. I also choose to forgive myself for _____*(insert every self-inflicted offense. Ex: not finishing school, having abortions)* I release myself into the freedom of my forgiveness in Jesus' name. Amen.

Step 6) Casting Out- This part of the process can get very interesting. It would be wise to have anointed oil napkins, paper towels, hand sanitizer, and plastic bags on hand, as demons cause many people to purge.

The first thing that you will do in your prayer is exalt God as the Lord who wars on our behalf and acknowledge Jesus as His Son who has all authority. Thank God for the person's legal ground being broken and then command every spirit that has been operating in their lives to leave them, in Jesus' name. Remember, you have the authority of heaven backing you. You don't have to yell or shout; simply make bold biblical declarations. Don't look for immediate manifestations. Just keep praying according to what you have identified during the interview. Remember, demons are never alone. Where there is one, there is a group of them. Ask Holy Spirit to lead you in what to call out of the person. Also, remember that you have the authority to tell demons where to go. I believe that it is appropriate to command them to go to the dry places, the feet of Jesus, or the foot of the cross. You cannot cast demons "back to the pits of hell from where they came" because they didn't come from there. If manifestations get out of control, revisit the interview questionnaire and legal ground prayers.

Guided "Casting Out" Prayer- Father, I thank You for being the Lord of all. I also thank You for the reality that all souls belong to You. I thank You that You are Jehovah Gibbor— the Lord who stands to defend His people. I thank You for being Jehovah Sabaoth who wars on behalf of His people. Father, I ask now that by the blood of Your Son Jesus that You would drive out every demonic spirit that has come to inflict _____ *(insert person's name)* life. Now, by the name of Jesus Christ and the power of Holy Spirit, I command every spirit that has entered _____ *(insert person's name)* life to come out of _____ *(insert person's name)* now. Come out of the skeletal system, come out of every portion of the brain, come out of the eyes, come out of the muscular system, come out of the……. *(Call out demons from* *any part of the body where you have seen through the interview or revelation of Holy Spirit.)*

At this point, you can begin to call out spirits by name. *(ex: Shame come out, fear come out, addiction come out, etc.)* Don't be afraid to repeat the names of spirits as you are led by Holy Spirit. Some spirits will come out instantly, but others will come out as you continue to call their names.

Step 7) Fill and Seal- After you feel the release from Holy Spirit, you should always pray a filling prayer. The release from Holy Spirit can feel different ways for different people, but the way I know that deliverance is done because the rooms feel light. Even if the person already says he/she has the gift of Holy Spirit, pray for a fresh filling in the areas that were once occupied by spirits. Another way you can fill areas is to prophesy over them. Encourage, exhort, and edify. After that, you will pray a sealing prayer.

Guided Sealing Prayer- Father, I thank You for the work that Your Holy Spirit has done in _____*(insert person's name)* today. I pray that _____ *(insert person's name)* be sealed by the blood of the Lamb. If any spirit returns to him/her, may it find him/her covered under the blood of the Lamb until the day Jesus returns. Amen.

After the session is complete, answer any questions the recipient may have. Encourage him/her to seek counseling and push him/her to submit to discipleship and accountability. It takes a village to walk out deliverance. There is safety in submission to Godly churches.

Virtual Deliverance Sessions

Virtual deliverance sessions have become a necessary alternative to in-person deliverance sessions due to the Covid-19 pandemic of 2020. Before the outbreak, people would fly to me from all over the world to receive deliverance ministry. It is a significant part of my ministry. I was skeptical about virtual deliverance sessions at first because I still felt like I needed to touch people in order for them to be free. However, the requests became overwhelming. I took it to God in prayer, and I was reminded of a powerful passage in Psalms.

Psalm 107:20 (KJV)

20 He sent his word, and healed them, and delivered them from their destructions.

I was also reminded of the time where Jesus sent his word to heal Jairus' daughter. It gave me the revelation that deliverance isn't about physically pushing spirits out of a person. It is about the person hearing and agreeing with the prayers being prayed to make the decision to be free.

The steps for virtual deliverance are identical to the steps for personal deliverance sessions. Here are some suggestions:

1. If you can't do the virtual sessions with someone else, make sure the session is recorded.
2. Ensure the person feels comfortable and knows that the recording will be sent to him/her and only to be used as a point of reference.
3. Also, it would be helpful for those receiving ministry to fill out a liability waiver and a questionnaire prior to the session.

Altar Deliverance Sessions

There is little to no time to allow the recipient to repeat your prayers during most altar sessions. Because of this, you will have to pray directly into his/her ear.

Step 1) Ask- If the leading minister doesn't make an altar call for a specific issue, you should ask the person how you can pray for him/her. Always start with what he/she asks for. If led by the Holy Spirit, begin to pray over other areas as well.

Step 2) Prayer Etiquette- While praying for a person at the altar, pray in English in his/her ears. Do not yell in tongues into his/her ear. He/she won't understand anything you say. With his/her permission, place your hand(s) on his/her shoulders or grab his/her hands and pray in your normal voice, so he/she can hear and understand you.

Step 3) Casting Out- If you feel led to call out spirits, make sure you clarify to the person that you are not talking to him/her. Tell him/her that you are speaking to every negative thing that has warred against him/her. If the lead minister has made a specific altar call, stay on track with what was called. Remember, you don't have much time so be strategic and effective.

Self-deliverance Sessions

Self-deliverance is a tool of soul care that every believer should practice. It's a discipline just like prayer, meditation, and fasting. We have been given authority over all the power of the enemy, and that authority is not just for other people. Paul encouraged the Philippians church to mature and work out their own soul salvation!

Philippians 2:12 (KJV)

12 Wherefore, my beloved, as ye have always obeyed, not as in my presence only, but now much more in my absence, work out your own salvation with fear and trembling.

In this passage. The Greek word used for salvation also translates to deliverance. In essence, Paul is saying that believers are responsible for the deliverance of their own mind, will, and emotions. Below I have listed some practical steps to take yourself through deliverance with Holy Spirit!

1. Partner with Holy Spirit for a time of self-reflection and assessment of the condition of your soul. Identify any active :

    a. Sin cycles

    b. Generational curses

    c. Word curses

    d. Trauma

    e. Soul ties

2. Make a list of the areas you need deliverance. Partner with Holy Spirit! Ask Him to help you see the areas you need deliverance and ask Him to show you the root of the issue. Common areas:

    a. Fear

    b. Rejection

    c. Abandonment

    d. Loneliness

    e. Anger

3. Research scriptures to counteract what's attacking you. Here are some examples.

    a. 2 Timothy 1:7

    b. Ephesians 1:5-7

    c. Deuteronomy 31:6

    d. Isaiah 41:10

    e. Colossians 3:15

4. Pray a rededication prayer to reestablish Jesus as Lord of your life.

5. Pray prayers that break legal ground.
    a. Repentance
    b. Renunciation
    c. Confession
    d. Forgiveness

6. Command every spirit that is not of God to leave your life!
    a. PRAY THE WORD! (revisit point 3)

7. Once you feel like you have freedom, ask Holy Spirit to renew, refresh, and refill you! Ask Him to speak or show you His plans for your life.

8. Thank Holy Spirit for helping you get freedom and make a verbal declaration that everything that left your life can't come back!

9. Repeat as needed.

Deliverance Don'ts

- Do not push someone down by pushing his/her head back. Lay hands on the shoulders. If you are led to lay hands anywhere else, always ask for permission. Please be careful not to touch people in sensitive areas.

- Do not administer deliverance without having consumed a mint or other breath freshener. Always have mints. Your breath should not be offensive to anyone you are praying for.
- Do not pray in tongues into the person's ear. Pray in tongues before you go to the altar. Pray in his/her native language in his/her ear.
- Do not yell into the person's ear. You don't want to distract him/her from receiving what you are praying.
- Do not blow into the person's face.
- Do not ask people for personal or sensitive information at the altar.
- Do not lay hands around the altar without permission from the leader.

Remember, personal deliverance sessions are much more intimate and can take a long time, but altar deliverance is much more surface and impersonal.

Chapter Eleven
Workbook Section

1. Follow the steps in chapter 11. Take yourself through self-deliverance. Write in the notes section about your experience.

_____

_____

_____

_____

_____

_____

_____

_____

_____

_____

_____

_____

2. Did you feel anything leave you as you prayed?

_____

_____

_____

_____

_____

_____

_____

_____

_____

_____

_____

_____

_____

_____

3. What did you feel leave your life?

_____

_____

_____

_____

_____

_____

_____

4. What will your approach be when taking someone else through deliverance?

_____

_____

_____

_____

_____

_____

_____

Exercise: In the notes section, name the variations of deliverance ministry styles and how they differ from each other.

_____

_____

_____

_____

_____

_____

_____

_____

_____

_____

_____

_____

_____

_____

Chapter Twelve
Demonic Snapshots

Many times in deliverance, Holy Spirit will give you the name of the "strong man." The strong man is the head of every demonic group. Calling the demon by its name, what it says, or how it manifests will kill any excuse the demon has to ignore your command. Demons are masters of secrecy and do not want to be exposed, but knowing their names can be instrumental in calling deliverance recipients into the light of freedom. I included a short list of demons you will commonly come across during deliverance sessions. This is not a complete list, so if you would like more information on certain spirits, I suggest reading the book titled *Demon Hit List* by Apostle John Eckhardt and *Setting The Captives Free* by Pastor Bev Tucker.

Demonic Snapshots

ABANDONMENT- occurs when someone relinquishes his/her responsibilities to another person or group of people. This spirit partners with loneliness, betrayal, isolation, rejection, and paranoia to make a person feel unwanted and unloved. Abandonment is often found in widows and people who grew up in broken homes. Counteract with Matthew 28:20; Song of Songs 7:10

ABORTION- a spirit that haunts women who terminate pregnancies. When a woman consents to abortion, she becomes a victim and a victimizer. It partners with murder, death, and premature death. Counteract with John 6:35; Ezekiel 16:6

ABUSE- is defined as "to misuse or to mishandle." This spirit can manifest in several ways physically, verbally, and emotionally. It partners with control, torment, criticism, resentment, and exploitation. Counteract with Luke 6:35

ACCUSATION- a major tool Satan uses against God's people. This spirit partners with scandal, slander, lying, gossip, and tale bearing. Counteract with Matthew 5:10-11

ADDICTION- a response to an obsession. Addiction manifests in a compulsive desire for substances or activities. It partners with compulsion, obsession, and slavery. Counteract with 1 Corinthians 10:13-14

ADULTERY- a spirit that works to bring shame to the family unit. It partners with Jezebel, division, dishonor, shame, and rejection.

ANGER- a spirit that can cause irrational thinking and acts of violence, if not controlled. It partners with rage, murder, wrath, and destruction. Counteract with Psalm 37:8-9

ANXIETY- an uneasy or distressed state of mind that partners with fear, hopelessness, depression, and worry. Counteract with Philippians 4:6

BARRENNESS- a common result after abortion. This spirit can cause sterility in women and men. It partners with fruitlessness, sterility, and uselessness. Counteract with Isaiah 54:1

BETRAYAL- a tool of dishonor that robs a person of his/her ability to trust. It partners with isolation, rejection, hurt, deep hurt, and anxiety. Counteract with Isaiah 26:3-4

BITTERNESS- the fruit of unforgiveness that partners with hatred, ill will, and malice. This can be a hindrance to deliverance if not released. Counteract with Ephesians 4:26

CAMOUFLAGE- a spirit of deception that tries to conceal motives. It partners with deception.

CONDEMNATION- a spirit that causes mental and emotional torment about past mistakes. This spirit is an enemy to deliverance. It partners with shame, guilt, accusation, and judgement. Counteract with Romans 8:1

CONFUSION- a spirit that comes to blind people from the revelation of God's word. It partners with false doctrine, chaos, idolatry and deception. Counteract with 1 Corinthians 14:33

CONTENTION- a spirit that thrives on heated argument and causes division. It partners with anger, pride, envy, and control. Counteract with Hebrews 12:14

CONTROL- the root of all witchcraft that partners with manipulation, possessiveness, and religion. Control is often used to direct a person's behavior and future. Counteract with Isaiah 41:10

DEATH- a spirit assigned to anointed vessels. The most deadly spirit in Satan's ranks. It partners with accidents, heart attacks, strokes, cancer, sickness and disease, murder, and abortion. Counteract with 1 Corinthians 15:54-55

DOUBT- a spirit of resistance against deliverance and freedom. It partners with unbelief, skepticism, and self-delusion. Counteract with Mark 9:23

DRUGS- a spirit that comes to alter reality, alleviate pain, fill voids, or numb trauma. Greek word: *pharmakeia,* meaning drugs or sorcery. It partners with heroin, marijuana rebellion, disobedience, hallucination, depressant, stimulants, narcotics, sedatives, antidepressants, and hypnotic. Counteract with 1 Peter 5:8

FALSE STRENGTH- a spirit that plays on the traumas of the past to cause a person to build up walls and self-defense mechanisms. It partners with grief, pride, orphan spirit, and abandonment. Counteract with Psalm 28:7

FAMILIAR SPIRITS- spirits that have contracts with the family and go from generation to generation. Familiar spirits can include divination, abuse, addiction, etc.

FEAR- a spirit that directly attacks our faith in God's ability, intentions, and love concerning us. It partners with apprehension and causes torment. Counteract with 1 Peter 5:6-7; Psalm 118:6, 2 Timothy 1:7

FORTUNE-TELLING- a spirit of divination that gives information collected by demonic spies. Participation can open the door to demonic torment. Fortune-telling uses clairvoyance, bone reading, tarot card reading, reading stars, and other tools forbidden by God.

GAMBLING- a spirit associated with compulsion and greed. Like any other addiction, it aims to destroy. Gambling breeds a form of covetousness. The tenth commandment admonishes us not to covet. It partners with covetousness, greed, and selfishness are the base emotions that entice us to gamble.

GRIEF- a spirit associated with the deep sorrow and sadness often associated with loss. It partners with anguish, heartache, and distress to lock a person into depression. Grief is a natural emotion, but when it is not processed properly, demonic forces can come to empower feelings of grief. Counteract with Psalm 34:18

HATRED- an intense dislike of another person or group of people, often to the point of ill wishes. It partners with anger, murder, and destruction to keep people bound in emotional instability. Counteract with Proverbs 10:12

HOMOSEXUALITY- this behavior undermines the biblical definition of family and marriage. It promotes stimulation without the ability to procreate. It partners with uncleanness, confusion, lust, and rebellion.

IDOLATRY- an affection towards any person or thing that takes the place of honor belonging to God. Partners with pride, Jezebel, and Baal.

INCEST- a spirit that causes sexual relations between close relatives. It partners with deep trauma, neurotic conditions, heinous criminal activities, and intergenerational dysfunctions. Counteract with 1 Thessalonians 5:23–24

INFIRMITY- a spirit commonly used by Satan to torment God's people. It directly attacks the faith in God as a healer. It partners with isolation, hopelessness, and fear of death. Counteract with Psalm 103:3

JEALOUSY- a spirit that is rooted in insecurity and aims to destroy relationships. It partners with envy, suspicion, and spite. Counteract with Philippians 2:3

JEZEBEL- a spirit that wars for power and control. It will use any form of manipulation to gain control. It partners with python, whoredom, false doctrine, and self-idolatry.

LAZINESS- a spirit that leads people into poverty. Partners with idleness, slothfulness, and drowsiness to keep a person from fulfilling his or her purpose. <u>Counteract with Proverbs 13:4</u>

LYING- one trait of every demon is lying. Even when they attempt to tell the truth, demons lie. There are some specific spirits that are assigned to lie. It partners with deception, manipulation, and control.

MOCKERY- a type of tormenting spirit that comes often to disrupt services and the movement of Holy Spirit. It partners with scorning, disdain, and disrespect.

MOLESTATION- a type of sexual abuse that opens the door for many other spirits to torment a person. Molestation often threatens and demands secrecy. It partners with predator spirits and torment.

MURDER- a spirit that can manifest in the form of word curses and ill will towards others. It partners with rage and anger. <u>Counteract with Exodus 20:13</u>

NARCISSISM- a prideful spirit that causes a person to be self-centered and apathetic. It causes destruction, strife, tension, and jealousy.

NIGHTMARE- a tormenting spirit that comes during sleep to cause anxiety or restlessness. It is often a result of unhealed hurts and unresolved issues.

OCCULT- the secretive, hidden, and mysterious. It includes witchcraft, sorcery, divination, ESP, hypnosis, fortune-telling, crystal ball, Ouija board, tarot cards, freemasonry, martial arts, magic, seances, clairvoyance, mediums, psychics, readers, advisors, necromancy, handwriting analysis, astrology, yoga, metaphysical healing groups, hypnotism, occult movies, occult programs, occult books, occult games, New Age movement, amulets, talismans, ankhs, yin yang, Eastern religions, transcendental meditation, and familiar spirits.

OPPRESSION- a spirit that totally ravishes the soul and leaves it wanting as it steals the dignity and quality of life. Proverbs 28:3, says this spirit is like a "sweeping rain which leaveth no food." It partners with heaviness, depression, affliction, and torment Counteract with Psalm 9:7-10

PAIN- tormenting spirits including headaches, migraines, mental pain (caused by octopus spirit of mind control), stomach pain, arthritis, rheumatism, back pain, neck pain. Pain spirits can operate throughout the body, loins (Isaiah 21:3). Perpetual (Jeremiah 15:18) affliction (Psalm 25:18), hurt, painful memories, and emotional pain.

PERFECTIONISM- a spirit that is born out of rejection. It partners with ego, vanity, frustration, and intolerance.

PERVERSION- a spirit of error that is contrary to what is right. It is persistent in doing what is wrong. It partners with arrogance, corruption, and lust.

PESSIMISM- a spirit of negativity that causes a person's perspective to be wrong about everything. It partners with doubt, unbelief, suspicion, hopelessness, discouragement, distrust, doom, and gloom.

PRIDE- Leviathan, arrogance, little pride, hidden pride, hardness of heart, stubbornness, rebellion, rejection, anger, rage, pride of (knowledge, success, color, race, position, power, culture, religion, family name), vanity, ego, self- righteousness, haughtiness, importance, judging, arrogance, self-importance, self- conceit, self-love, self-exaltation, superiority.

PYTHON- partners strongly with divination. It is a large constrictor. These spirits squeeze the life out of relationships, churches, etc. Also, it partners with Jezebel to control prophetic voices. <u>Counteract with Acts 16:16-18</u>

RAPE- an attack of sexual violence on the physical, psychological, and emotional parts of a human being. It partners with hurt, shame, humiliation, molestation, torment, suicide, and insanity.

REBELLION- the righteousness of Satan's kingdom. It partners with defiance, seduction hatred, suspicion, distrust, confrontation, and control. Counteract with Psalm 119:67

REGRET- a spirit that keeps a person connected to the past rather than living for the future. It partners with shame, fear, self-hate, and doubt. Counteract with Philippians 3:13

REJECTION- a spirit that causes a person to become stuck in the present and fear moving forward. It makes moving into covenant relationships difficult. Rejection can open the door for a multitude of spirits including rebellion, pride, bitterness, self-pity, escape, guilt, inferiority, insecurity, fear, and hopelessness. Counteract with Ephesians. 1:6

RELIGIOSITY- a very strong spirit that indoctrinates people into shame and secrecy. Religious spirits can be very hard to break. It partners with denominationalism, legalism, conservatism, intolerance, dogmatism, tradition, religious prejudice, division, deception, control, mysticism, religious pride, imbalance, idolatry, sectarianism, heresy, and false doctrine. Counteract with Matthew 6:10

RESISTANCE- a spirit that comes to block the truth, the word, Holy Spirit, salvation, deliverance, praise and worship, and prayer. During deliverance, this is one of the first spirits to start dealing with. It partners with stubbornness, hardness of heart, impediment, obstruction, fighting, and arguing.

SABOTAGE- a spirit rooted in anger that causes a person to act upon his/her ill intent toward another person. It partners with treachery, subversion, treason, mischief, hurt, and rebellion. Counteract with 2 Corinthians 11:14–15

SCHIZOPHRENIA- a spirit that comes to arrest the development of a person's true personality and replace it with rejection and rebellion, causing a split personality. It partners with double-mindedness, instability, and confusion. Counteract with Philippians 2:5-11

SHAME- a spirit that comes to make a person feel unworthy. It convinces a person to believe he/she is inadequate, bad, or unworthy. It partners with dishonor, hurt, embarrassment, scandal, reproach, fear, guilt, and condemnation. Counteract with Romans 8:26–29

SUICIDE- a spirit of death that comes to end a life before purpose is fulfilled. This spirit causes people to feel isolated so that they can be tormented without help. It partners with depression, gloominess, discouragement, death, murder, despondency, despair, hopelessness, death wish, insanity, madness, confusion, and rejection. <u>Counteract with Isaiah 26:3 and Philippians 4:7</u>

TRAUMA- a spirit that opens the door to other spirits including fears, hurt, and bitterness. It partners with calamity, catastrophe, trauma, shock, death, and destruction.

VAGABOND- a spirit that causes a person to be unstable or feel settled. It partners with roaming, nomad, vagrant, drifting, aimlessness, roving, poverty, and rejection.

VOODOO- in the Americas and the Caribbean, this spirit is thought to be a combination of various African, Catholic, and Native American traditions. It partners with sorcery, witchcraft, hoodoo, jinx, hex, vex, spell, incantation, conjuration, occult, and spiritism.

Chapter Twelve
Workbook Section

List the ten demonic snapshots that have affected your life the most. In the notes section, write out a prayer (using scripture) to combat each of these spirits.

_____

_____

_____

_____

_____

_____

_____

_____

_____

_____

_____

_____

50 Deliverance Facts & Scriptures

Psalm 34:17 When the righteous cry for help, the Lord hears and delivers them out of all their troubles.

Psalm 107:6 Then they cried to the Lord in their trouble, and he delivered them from their distress.

"Remember, you share your authority with whatever you come into agreement with."

Psalm 50:15 "And call upon me in the day of trouble; I will deliver you, and you shall glorify me."

2 Samuel 22:2 He said, "The Lord is my rock and my fortress and my deliverer."

"The enemy's tactics have not changed at all. He is still deceiving people into believing the opposite of what God has said. He knows that if he can keep us deceived, he can keep us defeated!"

Psalm 34:4 I sought the Lord, and he answered me and delivered me from all my fears.

1 Corinthians 6:18 Flee from sexual immorality. Every other sin a person commits is outside the body, but the sexually immoral person sins against his own body.

"Demon's ability to affect you solely depends on what you allow them to do. Remember, Christ gave us power over them!"

1 John 2:20 But you have been anointed by the Holy One, and you all have knowledge.

2 Chronicles 20:17 You will not need to fight in this battle. Stand firm, hold your position, and see the salvation of the Lord on your behalf, O Judah and Jerusalem. Do not be afraid and do not be dismayed. Tomorrow go out against them, and the Lord will be with you.

"You must never show sympathy to any demon. It is your job to call them out so the person can be set free; they are NOT your friends."

2 Chronicles 7:14 If my people who are called by my name humble themselves, and pray and seek my face and turn from their wicked ways, then I will hear from heaven and will forgive their sin and heal their land.

2 Peter 2:9 Then the Lord knows how to rescue the godly from trials, and to keep the unrighteous under punishment until the day of judgment.

"When God needed a body to do his work among men he created one! Satan doesn't have that kind of authority."

2 Samuel 22:1 And David spoke to the Lord the words of this song on the day when the Lord delivered him from the hand of all his enemies, and from the hand of Saul.

2 Thessalonians 3:3 But the Lord is faithful. He will establish you and guard you against the evil one.

"Suspicion judges the person. Discerning of Spirit judges the enemy of that person's soul!"

2 Timothy 3:16 All Scripture is breathed out by God and profitable for teaching, for reproof, for correction, and for training in righteousness.

Acts 10:38 How God anointed Jesus of Nazareth with the Holy Spirit and with power. He went about doing good and healing all who were oppressed by the devil, for God was with him.

"Satan is a legalist which means that for him to take a space, he must have an agreement with the person who owns it. You are in charge of your own mental space."

Colossians 1:13 He has delivered us from the domain of darkness and transferred us to the kingdom of his beloved Son.

Exodus 14:13 And Moses said to the people, "Fear not, stand firm, and see the salvation of the Lord, which he will work for you today. For the Egyptians whom you see today, you shall never see again."

"Broken boundaries lead to tied souls!"

Galatians 5:1 For freedom Christ has set us free; stand firm therefore, and do not submit again to a yoke of slavery.

Genesis 17:1 When Abram was ninety-nine years old the Lord appeared to Abram and said to him, "I am God Almighty; walk before me, and be blameless."

"Forgiveness is not about a feeling. When you choose to forgive a person, you must then command your emotions to align with your decision."

Genesis 45:7 And God sent me before you to preserve for you a remnant on earth, and to keep alive for you many survivors.

Isaiah 43:13 "Also henceforth I am he; there is none who can deliver from my hand; I work, and who can turn it back?"

"Demonic manifestations are not something that you take time to analyze or gaze at with awe."

Isaiah 61:3 To grant to those who mourn in Zion— to give them a beautiful headdress instead of ashes, the oil of gladness instead of mourning, the garment of praise instead of a faint spirit; that they may be called oaks of righteousness, the planting of the Lord, that he may be glorified.

James 4:7 Submit yourselves therefore to God. Resist the devil, and he will flee from you.

"It takes a village to walk out deliverance."

James 5:16 Therefore, confess your sins to one another and pray for one another, that you may be healed. The prayer of a righteous person has great power as it is working.

John 1:1 "In the beginning was the Word, and the Word was with God, and the Word was God."

"Demons can only operate in areas of our lives that we allow them to. "

John 15:7 "If you abide in me, and my words abide in you, ask whatever you wish, and it will be done for you."

John 3:16 For God so loved the world, that he gave his only Son, that whoever believes in him should not perish but have eternal life.

"We are at war, and if you aren't fighting, you've already been captured.

John 8:32 "And you will know the truth, and the truth will set you free."

Luke 10:19 "Behold, I have given you authority to tread on serpents and scorpions, and over all the power of the enemy, and nothing shall hurt you."

"You must never forget that demons are not all-powerful. They can only do what we allow them to do."

Joel 2:32 And it shall come to pass that everyone who calls on the name of the Lord shall be saved. For in Mount Zion and in Jerusalem there shall be those who escape, as the Lord has said, and among the survivors shall be those whom the Lord calls.

Luke 4:18 "The Spirit of the Lord is upon me, because he has anointed me to proclaim good news to the poor. He has sent me to proclaim liberty to the captives and recovering of sight to the blind, to set at liberty those who are oppressed."

"The assignment against you individually is just a microcosm of the assignment of hell against your family! "

Luke 4:32 And they were astonished at his teaching, for his word possessed authority.

Luke 7:47 "Therefore I tell you, her sins, which are many, are forgiven—for she loved much. But he who is forgiven little, loves little."

"What empowers a word curse to be active in one's life is believing what's being said"

Mark 1:25 But Jesus rebuked him, saying, "Be silent, and come out of him!"

Mark 16:17 "And these signs will accompany those who believe: in my name they will cast out demons; they will speak in new tongues."

"There is safety in submission to Godly churches."

Matthew 10:1 And he called to him his twelve disciples and gave them authority over unclean spirits, to cast them out, and to heal every disease and every affliction.

Philippians 1:6 And I am sure of this, that he who began a good work in you will bring it to completion at the day of Jesus Christ.

"Words are vessels filled with spiritual power!"

Philippians 4:8 Finally, brothers, whatever is true, whatever is honorable, whatever is just, whatever is pure, whatever is lovely, whatever is commendable, if there is any excellence, if there is anything worthy of praise, think about these things.

Proverbs 28:13 Whoever conceals his transgressions will not prosper, but he who confesses and forsakes them will obtain mercy.

"One of the major open doors to mental torment is unforgiveness."

Psalm 10:12 Arise, O Lord; O God, lift up your hand; forget not the afflicted.

Psalm 107:20 He sent out his word and healed them, and delivered them from their destruction.

"Families are the most potent representation of God's kingdom! This is why Satan takes so much pleasure in seeing destruction woven into our bloodline through generational curses."

Psalm 18:17 He rescued me from my strong enemy and from those who hated me, for they were too mighty for me.

Psalm 32:7 You are a hiding place for me; you preserve me from trouble; you surround me with shouts of deliverance. Selah.

"It is irresponsible of you to cast the demon out of someone who doesn't agree or understand."

Psalm 40:13 Be pleased, O Lord, to deliver me! O Lord, make haste to help me!

Psalm 40:17 As for me, I am poor and needy, but the Lord takes thought for me. You are my help and my deliverer; do not delay, O my God!

"Prayer is not only the way that we communicate with God, but it is also the way we become sensitive to what God is saying and doing."

Psalm 40:2 He drew me up from the pit of destruction, out of the miry bog, and set my feet upon a rock, making my steps secure.

Psalm 51:17 The sacrifices of God are a broken spirit; a broken and contrite heart, O God, you will not despise.

"When we pray, our hearts become knit with God's heart! "

Romans 10:13 For "Everyone who calls on the name of the Lord will be saved."

Romans 5:8 But God shows his love for us in that while we were still sinners, Christ died for us.

"Bitterness, unforgiveness, pride, and dishonesty can be hindrances to freedom."

Romans 8:6 For to set the mind on the flesh is death, but to set the mind on the Spirit is life and peace.

Zechariah 9:11 As for you also, because of the blood of my covenant with you, I will set your prisoners free from the waterless pit.

"Soul ties are created through intimacy, and intimacy is more than sex. Intimacy is letting a person into your goals, apprehensions, and struggles."

ABOUT THE AUTHOR

Torace D. Solomon is a third-generation pastor and prophetic strategist with over a decade of church leadership experience. He is a resident of Atlanta, Georgia where he serves as Assistant Pastor at All Nations Worship Assembly Atlanta. He matriculated through bible college and holds a degree in Christian education. Torace is passionate about seeing believers equipped for the work of ministry and has a unique anointing that draws people out of places of potential, thrusting them into places of purpose through training and impartation. He is an accomplished author and sought after preacher with many testimonies of healing, miracles, and deliverance. His teachings hit obstacles at their core, bring light to dark places, and create life to dead situations. Torace is widely known for building leadership staff, training ministry teams, and activating the saints into deliverance ministry! He travels as a trainer, clinician, and consultant to help leaders fulfill their God-appointed destinies.

Made in the USA
Coppell, TX
30 July 2023